Horses
Forever

Horses Forever

Lawrence Scanlan

Scholastic Canada Ltd.

Scholastic Canada Ltd.
123 Newkirk Road, Richmond Hill, Ontario, Canada L4C 3G5

Scholastic Inc.
555 Broadway, New York, NY 10012, USA

Scholastic Australia Pty Limited
PO Box 579, Gosford, NSW 2250, Australia

Scholastic New Zealand Limited
Private Bag 94407, Greenmount, Auckland, New Zealand

Scholastic Ltd.
Villiers House, Clarendon Avenue, Leamington Spa,
Warwickshire CV32 5PR, UK

Cover photo by Kathi Lamm/Tony Stone Images

Back cover photo by Marilyn Kelley

Designed by Andrea Casault

Canadian Cataloguing in Publication Data
Scanlan, Lawrence
Horses forever
ISBN 0-590-12448-X
1. Horses — Juvenile literature. I. Title.
SF302.S32   1998   j636.1   C97-932417-3

5 4 3 2 1   Printed in Canada   8 9/9 0 1 2 /0

For David Carpenter,
who discovered horses long before I did

My sincere thanks:

To Sandra Bogart Johnston for her wise editing and to all at Scholastic Canada Ltd. for bringing the book to life.

To Ulrike Bender, David Carpenter, Laura Nacu and Kurt Scanlan for their careful reading of the manuscript.

To Jan Whitford, surely the most diligent literary agent in the land.

To Cindy Fisher, who gave me stories, loaned me books, and, best of all, encouraged me.

To all the riders, young and old, who wrote me letters and stories about their horses and ponies.

To Elizabeth Atwood Lawrence. *His Very Silence Speaks* (Wayne State University Press, 1989), illuminates Comanche the horse.

To Maxine Kumin. *In Deep* (Viking, 1987) lyrically captures the pull of the horse, and, especially, of horses of your own.

To Vicki Hearne. *Adam's Task* (HarperPerennial, 1994) and *Animal Happiness* (HarperCollins, 1994) make perfect horse sense.

To Aime Felix Tschiffely. *Tschiffely's Ride* (Simon & Schuster, 1933) still inspires seventy-two years later.

To Barbara Whittome, who rode the long and winding road. (*Russian Ride*, Boxtree, 1996).

To Monty Roberts, *The Man Who Listens to Horses* (Random House, 1997). He let me into his house and even into his head, that I might see how *he* sees horses.

To Dick and Adele Rockwell, and to Jim Elder, for that day in praise of ponies and jumpers.

To Susan Jayne Anstey for pointing the way.

To Bernard McCormack for the tour of Windfields Farm.

To Ruth Honeyman of the Canadian Pony Club for taking the time.

To Robin Brown at CBC Radio's "The Inside Track" for kindness to an erstwhile producer.

To Maria Simpson and Jessica Clarke, for their insights into horses and disabled riders.

To Skip Ashley of Lander, Wyoming, for taking me where the wild horses roam.

To Velma Johnston ("Wild Horse Annie") for getting there first, before the mustangers did.

And to the countless writers, cowboys, historians, librarians, journalists, photographers, adventurers, storytellers and riders green or grizzled who were drawn, as I was, to the glories of the horse.

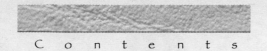

C o n t e n t s

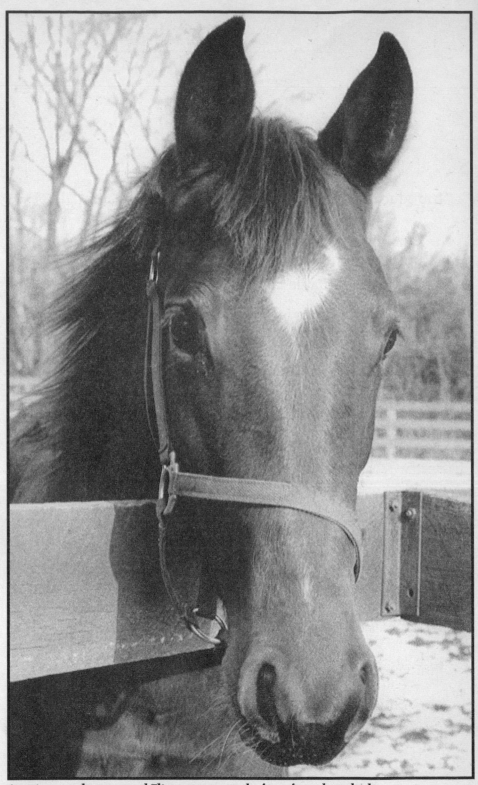

A curious racehorse named Flirt comes up to the fence for a closer look.
(Marilyn Kelley)

Introduction

Gallop even once in the open and you will instantly understand why humans have been connecting with horses for more than 6,000 years. But what lies at the heart of this age-old — and now growing — attraction to horses? Why do some people never get over that first stage of horse fever?

The answer might lie with the horses themselves. Horses like Colonel, a sorrel draft horse who lived on a Minnesota farm in the early 1900s. In summer, the kids on the farm would hitch Colonel to a box-like sled, then pile in. The huge horse with the white blaze down his long nose would turn to face the giggling crew, as if to say "Everyone safely on board?" There were no reins, no need of them. Colonel knew the routine. The kids would shout "Let's go, Colonel!" He would pull them across a wooden bridge that spanned a creek, but sometimes — maybe out of mischief — he would haul them into the creek, stopping for a long cool drink while they squealed with delight as the cold water flowed over their legs.

Colonel always seemed to know when someone had fallen out. Perhaps he heard the sound of a tiny body tumbling into the grass, perhaps he felt the load lighten a touch. He would stop, the massive head would swing around, and he would proceed only when all were safely seated.

It was the custom in those days to stable the horses all winter long. But in the spring, when the smell of new grass wafted in, the plough horses grew restless for the pasture. It became a ritual to release the horses all at once. Everyone on the farm would stop to look on as the great wing-gates to the pasture were opened and the herd was allowed to stampede out of the barn.

Down by the gate with the farm folk stood Colonel — no mere horse, after all, but one of the family. No one had noticed that little Eleanor was not with the rest of them, but on the other side of the gate. The moment that the farmers were slapping horses' flanks inside the barn and letting the animals stampede out was the moment that four-year-old Eleanor chose to cross in front of them. Her family froze, terrified.

Colonel bolted forward, bent one knee and knocked the little girl to the ground, then straddled her and faced the oncoming herd. An instant later the thundering horses sped round him, like water around a high rock in a brook, and galloped on to the pasture. Colonel leaned down and nuzzled Eleanor, then stepped back as her mother took the girl in her arms.

What I like about the story is how it captures the two towering aspects of horses — the sense of danger, because horses *are* big and strong and fast, and also their generosity of spirit. Anyone who has spent a life with horses has tales to tell about that generosity.

Cut from the same cloth as Colonel is Big Ben, the legendary Canadian show jumper now retired after more than a decade of competition. Often distant and cool with adults

**Draft horses like this pair, competing at a fall fair, are incredibly strong.
(Marilyn Kelley)**

he does not know, he will lower his great head to let a small child pat him. The tall chestnut and his tiny admirers seem to see eye to eye. Naturally, instinctively, Big Ben cherishes kids and seems to watch over them like some gentle giant.

Children struggling with life-threatening diseases sometimes have one final wish: to see and touch that horse. One girl with cancer wanted to ride him. But Ben's rider, Ian Millar, was cautious. Even he finds Ben a challenge to handle, and he's one of the world's top riders. But Ben seemed to know he had to be gentle with this girl. A photograph records the moment: Ian holding the reins, the horse as docile as an old pony, the girl beaming with delight.

If you love horses, or one horse in particular, have you ever asked yourself why?

Maybe it starts with awe. The horse you ride might weigh ten times as much as you. In size and strength, the animal could easily take charge. Yet when you ask the horse to canter (assuming your skill and the horse's good manners), he does it. He *listens*. And that's another reason why people love horses.

The bond between horse and human is usually first felt in childhood. That's where it all starts. Talk to older riders and trainers about the horses of their youth and you will be astonished at how they can call up long-gone horses — their names, their characters, detailed stories about them. We do remember the horses of childhood; they do touch us in meaningful ways.

And it seems that more and more young people want some sort of connection with ponies and horses. In thirty-three countries around the world, half a million kids belong to Pony Clubs, and the number is growing. In Canada alone there are more than 600,000 horses and over 3,000 commercial riding

Some days just watching a horse running through a meadow can make your spirits lift. (Rick Buncombe)

establishments. In the United States, the number of horses is 7 million; around the world it's 60 million.

You would think that our interest in horses would wane now that they serve no practical purpose. But the opposite is true. There are more horses in North America now than there were in the 1800s when horses powered the family farm. More younger people and adults are riding than ever before. Vacation might be a week at a riding camp for kids, or the whole family riding at a guest ranch in the Canadian or American West. The age of the computer has also become, in a very real way, the age of the horse.

Most younger people tend to like animals in general. But this feeling for horses is something else. The word obsession often describes it perfectly. It's like you belong to a club, and only other members of the club know how you feel.

How do you explain this depth of feeling for horses? Some days your spirit can lift just watching a horse gracefully lifting his hoofs in a trot, or cantering over a hilltop.

Anne St. Martin knows the feeling. She trades barn chores at her local stable for riding privileges. Anne had a great affection for a Grand Prix horse called Jack, a horse with uncommon power, speed and athletic gifts. She spent ten months working around Jack. He had come from a large stable where no one could ride him without a fight. By degrees, Anne got closer to him. Groomed him. Slipped him a carrot or two. Jack visibly calmed in her presence, and despite Anne's limited experience, she rode him at her instructor's invitation. That summer she rode him every day. "We developed a bond," she says, "and a trust in each other that is simply too complicated to explain. I was his angel and he was my wings."

That might sound a little dramatic, but it reflects the special bond people have with horses. "The best thing for the inside of a person," an old saying goes, "is the outside of a horse."

Like a rope with two strands interwoven, the history of humankind is intertwined with the history of the horse. It's why a person like Ian Millar used to sit astride a piano bench as a boy, and gallop an invisible horse — when he should have been practising Bach concertos. It's why kids trade hours of work mucking out stalls, just to be around horses. They have the fever.

Happily — something I've come to know ever since I've been around horses — for this fever there is no known cure.

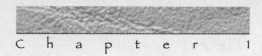
Horsing Around Through the Ages

What do wine, sparrow eggs, bread, camel milk and sheep fat have in common? All were fed, from time to time throughout history, to horses. It is a puzzling and amusing aspect of our long association with horses. You'd think we would have come to some basic understanding of them, and realize that horses prefer oats, say, to oysters.

Primitive humans began to domesticate the horse some 30,000 years ago, and began to ride the horse in what is now Ukraine 6,000 years ago. Even before inventing the wheel, some clever (and brave) human invented riding. By fits and starts, we figured out horses. But progress was often slow.

Think of it. For thousands of years humans rode horses — without stirrups. The Huns of what we now call Asia devised the stirrup about 1,500 years ago. It's a good feeling to ride a horse bareback, to feel the horse's body so directly, but imagine riding like that into war.

9

In Roman Times

Two thousand years ago there lived a Roman emperor named Gaius Caesar Germanicus (A.D. 12–41). Behind his back they called him Caligula (in Latin it means "Little Boots," for he often wore *caligae* or soldier's boots). When we think of the decline of the Roman empire, we think of Caligula. He was, in a word, nuts. Keener on games and horses than in actually managing the realm, he built a huge amphitheatre and filled it with water so that mock naval battles could be held as entertainments. Little boys play war in their bathtubs; Caligula used his fabulous wealth to build a vast bathtub and bleachers — the watery SkyDome of its day.

He was also mad about horses, and one in particular, a horse who competed in the chariot races. He was called Incitatus, or "spurred on." Caligula actually made Incitatus a citizen of the Roman empire. He gave the horse a gem-studded collar, had a horse blanket made of royal purple (the emperor's colour), and gave him oats dipped in gold (which can't have been good for the horse's teeth!). In a stable of marble, eighteen servants waited on Incitatus. They fed him — or tried to, anyway — the things that Caligula thought he would enjoy: mice dipped in butter, raw mussels, marinated squid.

Caligula then promoted the horse from citizen to priest, and held a special banquet to mark the occasion. Distinguished senators arrived to find Incitatus on his haunches seated on a chair and wearing his jewels and a white bib. But when a platter of roast chicken was presented to the horse, Incitatus spooked, upsetting the table and sending everyone fleeing.

Caligula was soon assassinated — the fate of many ancient kings and emperors. Incitatus went back to being a mere horse.

The New World

Almost 1,500 years later, when the people of the New World first saw the horses that Europeans had brought to their shores, they felt only terror. South Americans who saw a Spanish conquistador in full plate armour thought that horse and rider were one creature. Upon seeing the rider dismount, they thought the creature had come apart.

Outnumbered thousands to one, the Spaniards naturally encouraged the native inhabitants to see the horses as gods capable of terrible fury and revenge. In one battle an entire army of warriors fled from just twelve Spanish cavalrymen — monsters, they thought, with human faces. The people viewed horses with such awe that some of them even rubbed horse sweat on their bodies in a vain attempt to acquire the power of the horse.

In one skirmish, a proud black horse named Morzillo was struck in the mouth by an arrow. His rider, the Spanish commander Hernan Cortés , also took an arrow in the hand. Mad with pain, and angry too, Morzillo furiously attacked the enemy. He kicked and bit, and the Aztecs panicked at his onslaught.

When peace had been restored, and Morzillo had sufficiently healed from the arrow wound, Cortés left the horse with people near the town of Tayascal. They said they could heal a splinter in the horse's foot, and were perhaps pleased to be entrusted with the care of a creature they revered. They named him Tziminchac — god of thunder and lightning.

To appease him, they decorated Morzillo with flowers and put before him their idea of delicacies — succulent fruit and cooked chicken. Poor Morzillo. He must have missed his master, and he cannot have thrived on this new diet. He wasted away and died.

A century later two Spanish priests arrived in the same town. Inside a huge temple the priests saw the statue of a horse seated on his haunches. By no means forgotten, El Morzillo had become an idol — and so revered that the Spanish priests who smashed the statue to pieces were lucky to escape with their lives.

The Dawn Horse

When Columbus first brought horses to the New World in the fifteenth century, they were actually coming *back* to the land of their ancestors, for horses evolved in North America some 54 million years ago. The first version of the horse was a little dog-like creature that anthropologists now call *Hyracotherium* or *Eohippus* — the "dawn horse." Over time, as the climate changed and got drier, the forests gave way to grassland in the centre of the continent. And while Incitatus and Morzillo may have been fed chicken, it is grass, of course, that horses really love.

As the savannah grew more lush, the dawn horse got bigger. He could no longer hide from his enemies in the forest; he became a creature of flight, and his legs grew longer. His several toes evolved into one toe — a hoof. Over time the dawn horse's teeth changed to handle this new vegetation: not leaves and fruit anymore, but grass. He would need powerful front teeth to clip the grass, and molars at the back to chew it. To make room for all these cheek teeth, the horse's face grew longer. The eyes set on the side of his head gave him 360-degree vision to spot his enemies.

The result was *Equus*, the horse we know today. *Equus* thrived on the great plains, then a seemingly endless pasture. Some horses crossed over to what is now Europe and Asia, using land bridges that no longer exist. But about

15,000 years ago all the horses in North America — along with camels, sabre-toothed cats and mastodons — disappeared. No one is sure why. Was it climate change? Or did primitive humans hunt them to extinction? For thousands of years, our continent was horseless.

Meanwhile, on the plains of Russia, these primitive horses continued to survive. But here, too, they were a source of food long before they were ever tamed or ridden. Near a French village, scientists have found a metre-deep layer of horse bones stretching over a vast area. The remains of some 100,000 horses lie here. Their skins would have kept humans warm, their dung would have fuelled fires, their flesh would have saved humans from starvation.

But just because these early humans ate horses does not mean they didn't admire them or hold them in awe. Cave paintings of horses in France are probably 15,000 years old, and are remarkable for their colour, style and fluid motion. We have not stopped painting, or admiring, horses since.

In time horse slaughter turned to horse sacrifice. A nobler, higher calling for *Equus*. The end, sadly, was the same for the unfortunate horse chosen to appease the gods. But soon the horse was pulling carts and chariots, then being ridden. The horse gained stature, as did any human who rode a horse. Eventually the horse became too valuable to sacrifice. It was both a source of meat and a weapon in war — so valuable that an early pope even declared a taboo on eating horseflesh.

Thus elevated in rank, the horse got better treatment than any other domesticated animal, and his human owners showed appreciation by — once again — giving him odd things to eat. Horse fare through the ages has included beer, curry and oysters. In ancient India horses got vegetables dipped in honey, and on military campaigns, wine to calm them. The Romans offered their horses a supplement of sparrow eggs, and maintained hospitals called *veterinaria* for sick and wounded horses.

Arabs in the desert fed their horses dates, and the horses learned to spit out the pits. (Pitooey!) In cold weather Arabs also brought their horses into the tent, and when water was scarce the foals got camel's milk.

Ancient Siberians started young horses on salted fish; older horses got raw meat. Two seventeenth-century French noblemen hoping to spark their horses before a race fed them 300 eggs each!

During all this time humans were learning more and more about how to train a horse, and how to ride a horse well. Many cultures would become horse cultures. The Greeks, Romans, Germans, Huns and Hungarians would all, at various periods in history, lay claim to being the best horsemen in the world.

In the fourteenth century Europeans began to see riding as an art form. An educated person, especially from one of the higher classes, was expected to learn art, music and literature, of course. But he or she also had to learn the finer points of horsemanship. Elegant riding schools so lavish they looked like opera houses sprang up all over Europe.

The Horse in the New World

While the perfumed upper classes were riding sleek horses in the Old World, Christopher Columbus was bringing some of those same fine horses to the New World. The very first horses who came in 1494 were less fine: in fact, they were broken-down nags. It seems that before boarding ship the officers sold the purebred steeds they were supposed to bring, in order to buy wine. What little money remained was used to buy the nags. Only six survived that harsh journey. Crammed into small ships, the horses were suspended from the ceilings of the lower decks with straps under their bellies.

Worse, ships travelling to the New World were sometimes becalmed north and south of the equator. For days they would drift lazily on the currents under a blazing sun. When water supplies ran out and the horses went mad with thirst, sailors tossed them overboard. Today we still call those areas the Horse Latitudes.

More horses, and better ones, did arrive in the New World, and the last thing the conquering Spanish wanted was for the tribes they were enslaving to learn horsemanship. But there was no keeping the horse genie in the bottle. Native South Americans employed as grooms soon learned to ride, and horses escaped into the wild. *Mestenos*, the Spanish called them — horses without owners. Americans heard *mestenos* and thought mustang was easier to say. The mustangs headed north, to the plains where their ancestors had grazed and flourished millions of years before.

By the 1700s the Native Americans on the prairie had tamed enough mustangs to become "lords of the plains. The Blackfoot, the Crow, the Comanche and many other tribes had become, in short order, what the U.S. Cavalry battling them in the 1800s would call "the finest light cavalry in the world." By the time they were only six or seven years old, Blackfoot boys and girls were formidable riders. One colonel in the U.S. cavalry described the twelve- to fifteen-year-old Plains boy as "the best rough rider and natural horseman in the world." These boys could ride their ponies bareback at a full gallop and reach down to sweep up an object from the ground. They would gallop in pairs to a friend standing on the ground, lift him up onto one horse and take him away without pause.

The horse lay at the very heart of the Plains Indian culture. The horse was the measure of their wealth, the margin of victory in war, the difference between life and death in the ever-dangerous buffalo hunt. In the Crow culture, if you wanted to insult someone, you hit his horse in the face. In the early 1800s, the Comanches owned huge numbers of horses: a band might possess 6,000 head and a chief many hundreds. They traded horses all over the plains, and stole them with abandon. Horses were fiercely guarded, so such thefts took considerable courage and brought honour to any who succeeded.

Plains warriors could sometimes be hard on ordinary horses. But the prized buffalo horse or war horse was held in high esteem. An American army captain once offered a lot of money for the favourite horse of Sanaco, a Comanche chief. Sanaco declined to sell his buffalo horse, saying his people might suffer if he did. Besides, he said, stopping to pat the pony on the neck, "I love him very much."

Small wonder that a good horse had a place in a warrior's teepee, as it did in an Arab's tent. Small wonder that in the Old West the punishment for stealing a horse was death by hanging.

"I do not dream of things I eat," a Stoney man once told his interpreter a century or more ago. "I dream of horses."

Native Americans often took great pride in their ponies. © Edward Curtis (First Light)

Horses and Humans through History

Egyptians use
horses in battle,
shooting arrows
from chariots

1700 B.C.

4000 B.C.

Circa 340 B.C.

Alexander the
Great tames
Bucephalus

People in what is
now the Ukraine
begin to ride
horses

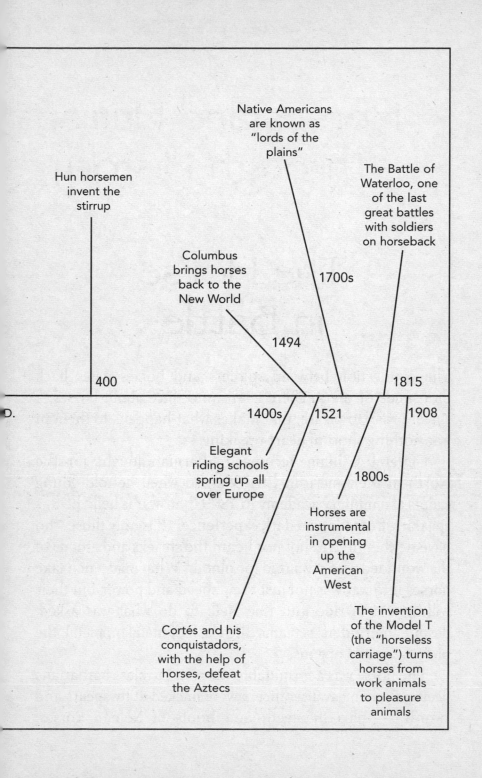

D.

Hun horsemen invent the stirrup

Native Americans are known as "lords of the plains"

The Battle of Waterloo, one of the last great battles with soldiers on horseback

Columbus brings horses back to the New World

1700s

400

1494

1815

1400s | 1521 | 1908

Elegant riding schools spring up all over Europe

1800s

Horses are instrumental in opening up the American West

Cortés and his conquistadors, with the help of horses, defeat the Aztecs

The invention of the Model T (the "horseless carriage") turns horses from work animals to pleasure animals

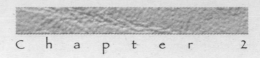
The Horse in Battle

The connection between soldiers and horses dates back thousands of years. There is an innocence about horses, a sincere wish to please, that makes what happens to them in war nothing short of heart-breaking.

General William Tecumseh Sherman fought for the North in the American Civil War, so when he told young cadets at a military academy in 1879 that "war is hell," he was speaking from his own dark experience. "It is only those who have neither fired a shot nor heard the shrieks and groans of the wounded who cry aloud for blood." What made men take horses into war was not just their speed and power, but their willingness to ride into that hell: to do what was asked, despite their riders' screams, the clash of metal on metal, the piercing sound of guns.

The horse was a formidable warrior. Luckless barbarians fleeing Roman cavalry officers were hacked at by spears and swords — plus the teeth and hoofs of Roman horses.

Soldiers throughout human history could not have asked for a more generous or devoted ally than the horse.

Comanche

One warhorse stands out among the rest. He is Comanche, the lone survivor (on the soldiers' side) of "Custer's Last Stand," the Battle of the Little Big Horn in what was then called the Montana Territory.

Comanche was ridden by an Irish-born officer in the U.S. Seventh Cavalry, Myles Keogh. Captain Keogh called him Comanche, either because the horse was once wounded in a battle with Comanches or because the horse let out "a Comanche yell" when he took an arrow in the hip. But even wounded, Comanche brought Keogh back to camp, where the horse patiently allowed a farrier to pull out the arrow and dress the wound.

There would be many more arrows and bullets — for Comanche, for the foolhardy General George Armstrong Custer, and for all the other soldiers and horses under his command. The Sioux and Cheyenne warriors massed and waiting for Custer that day, June 25, 1876, counted it a great victory, the last of its kind. For the soldiers it was a shattering defeat. When troops arrived in the Valley of the Little Big Horn two days later, they found every one of the 276 soldiers dead, and every horse killed or gone — except Comanche.

Little Soldier, a seventeen-year-old Sioux who fought at Little Big Horn, later explained why that one horse was left. It seems that Captain Keogh had ordered his men to shoot their horses and use their bodies as cover. Keogh himself had not yet done that, maybe because he could not bear to. He was kneeling between Comanche's legs and shooting at his attackers when he finally died of bullet wounds. But he still

held Comanche's reins tightly in his hand, and the Sioux looking on believed it was dangerous to disturb such a potent connection between rider and horse, between the living and the dead. "No Indian," said Little Soldier, "would take that horse when a dead man was holding the rein."

By the time the cavalry got to him days later, the horse was dying from six bullet wounds. One soldier was tempted to end his misery, but two others put water in their hats and got Comanche to drink. It took time, but eventually he was nursed back to health.

From that point, Comanche led the life of a military hero. A proclamation was passed by Congress that he never again be ridden or even put to work. He was housed in a special stall and given several personal attendants, including a blacksmith named Gustave Korn, whom he adored.

Comanche had become a living legend, and what Comanche wanted, Comanche got. He developed a taste for the finer things. During his long recovery, he got a whiskey bran mash every second day, and he would often wander over to the canteen where the men offered him, and he willingly drank, buckets of beer. Comanche would turn over garbage cans foraging for treats, and would sometimes be seen with coffee grounds on his mouth, like a kid with a milk moustache.

No area was off-limits for this horse. He grazed lawns and gardens, where he developed a fondness for sunflowers. He would follow Korn around like a faithful puppy, and when the blacksmith went to call on a lady friend, the jealous horse would neigh until Korn came out of the house to lead him home.

After Comanche died in 1891, they stuffed him. It was many years before they put him in a glass case, and by that time thousands of visitors had come to the museum in Kansas just to see the horse, and touch him. Some could not resist taking a souvenir hair from Comanche's tail. All those awestruck visitors patting the horse's nose and rump, for good luck, had given him a sad, rumpled look. (Years later it was reported that so many tail hairs were plucked that the museum caretaker had secretly replaced the tail seven times.)

More Tales of Warriors and Their Horses

• In World War II there was a black polo pony at a veterinary hospital who could detect — long before soldiers could — the approach of aircraft. That alone is not unusual. But this mare could apparently distinguish between Allied and German bombers. If the planes were German, she would stop eating, throw up her head, and with ears erect stand perfectly still. She would listen, then stamp, paw and show signs of excitement. But if the planes were friendly, she calmly continued eating.

• Horse soldiers — many of them, anyway — developed a real affection for the horses they rode into war. In the American Civil War, men under cover of darkness would steal food for their horses, even though it meant risking their own lives. British cavalry diaries from the 1700s tell of one horse refusing to leave the spot where his rider was killed and buried.

• A former U.S. cavalry officer told of seeing his warhorse, Pig, years after leaving the army. The horse was now part of a six-horse team and looked miserable, but his old master lacked the money to buy him back. "I went up to him and petted him," the old soldier wrote. "He knew me alright. He nickered and looked at me as much as to say, 'Come on, please, Charlie, get me out of here.' I had ridden old Pig thousands of miles and more than once he saved my life. I pretty near cried when I saw him that time in the Black Hills."

• In the First World War some 1.5 million horses were used as cavalry alone; 500,000 died. The diaries of cavalry officers paint a bleak picture of muddy battlefields where grooming ceased and a skin disease called mange spread among the horses like wildfire. To control it, the army had all horses clipped, but then they shivered in the cold. Water troughs froze, food supplies dwindled. Ravenous horses chewed on halters and blankets, even the manes and tails of other horses.

With few exceptions, horses sent to war in Europe did not come home. Survivors were sold, often to butchers in war-ravaged countries desperate for food. Even in death, the horses served.

Early War Horses

The horse was first used in war 4,000 years ago. Someone with imagination must have looked upon the donkey-drawn wagon and come up with the tank of its day — the horse-drawn two-man chariot. One man drove the horses, the other shot the arrows. Several thousand chariots at a time would charge at the enemy, and in minutes could inflict terrible damage on foot-soldiers. The chariot, though, was only useful on roads and flat plains. Mountains and rivers seriously impeded their progress.

By 700 B.C. the Huns had truly made the horse a partner in battle. Hun cavalry could cover almost 150 kilometres in a day. Each rider took a string of horses on conquering journeys that sometimes spanned thousands of kilometres.

When one horse tired, the rider mounted a fresh one, and the rest would follow like a pack of well-trained dogs. Huns were also amazingly adept at shooting arrows from the saddle, a skill that gave them a huge advantage over their enemies.

In time of need, the Hun horseman would make a delicate cut in the neck of his horse and drink a glass of blood, apparently without seriously harming the animal. The Hun warrior was as kind to his horse as he was unmerciful to his enemies, and the reward for old warhorses was retirement to a good pasture.

Hun warriors were such excellent horsemen that they overwhelmed the Chinese, who still used chariots and short swords. Even after switching to Hun tactics, the Chinese were never as brilliant on horseback as the Huns. In the end, the Chinese decided that the best offence was a good defence. The Great Wall of China was built, in part, to keep the Huns and their horses out.

The Middle Ages

The knights of the Middle Ages were as slow and heavy as the Huns were light and fast. Armoured knights rode one lighter horse to the site of the battle, and a much heavier horse when charging the enemy. Between the knight, his armour and the weight of saddle, stirrups and other tack, the poor horse had to bear a total weight of about 220 kilograms. Horses who could carry such a heavy load were far larger and stronger than today's typical saddle horse.

By the 1300s the invention of gunpowder introduced cannonballs, and eventually, artillery. Riding horses toward cannon was madness, which does not mean men stopped doing it right away, but eventually they did. The horse was still used in war, but more to move guns than to move men.

One of the last great battles involving soldiers on horseback was the Battle of Waterloo in 1815. Two horses from that epic battle, which featured a staggering 30,000 horses, are still remembered.

Marengo

Napoleon Bonaparte, the French commander at Waterloo, loved to ride greys, but that also made him a more obvious target for enemy fire. During his long military career, twenty horses were shot out from under him. The most famous, who survived Waterloo, was Marengo.

Like Bonaparte, he was small — a bit more than fourteen hands high. (A hand is four inches, just over ten centimetres.) Marengo was named after a village in Italy where Napoleon had won a decisive victory. What Napoleon admired about the horse was his steadiness amidst the chaos of battle. Throughout his life as a warhorse, Marengo would be wounded eight times, the last time at Waterloo.

He was an Arab, a muscled grey with a black mane. The story is told that he once saved the emperor's life. Napoleon and his horse were alone walking in the woods, the rider on foot and deep in thought, when suddenly Marengo stiffened, snorted and pointed his ears. Heeding his horse's warning, Napoleon leapt into the saddle and galloped off. The enemy spies who had been hiding in the bushes, ready to ambush him, couldn't catch Marengo — and Napoleon survived.

After Waterloo, the victorious English took Marengo back home with them, where he lived in luxury at a breeding farm and outlived his master by ten years, finally dying in 1831.

"1814" (Napoleon on Horseback) painting by Meissonier. (The Bettmann Archive)

Copenhagen

Across the battlefield at Waterloo that day in 1815 was a fifteen-hand chestnut originally trained as a racehorse, and ridden by the British commander, the Duke of Wellington. Wellington was known as the Iron Duke; his horse was Copenhagen.

Copenhagen was remarkable for his stamina and spirit. The day before the Battle of Waterloo, Wellington rode him for ten hours, and then from dawn to dusk on the day of the battle itself. When an exhausted Wellington finally lifted his body out of the saddle, Copenhagen swung around and aimed a kick that almost killed the Duke. Next day came more mischief: the fiery horse escaped his grooms and had to be chased through the streets of Brussels.

British soldiers loved him. Painters and sculptors set down his likeness, and so much was written about him that he became almost as famous as his master. When it came time, the Duke buried his horse with full military honours.

Never Say Die

For some bizarre reason, certain soldiers have an odd way of recognizing their horses' achievements. Some old soldiers can't bring themselves to bury their old warhorses in the ground. Horse remains become horse monuments — like Comanche. General Philip H. Sheridan rode a horse called Winchester in the American Civil War, and so grateful was the general that when Winchester died he had him done up like a big game trophy and presented to a war museum. Winchester is still on display today at the Smithsonian Institution in Washington.

Another American general, Robert E. Lee, fought for the South in the Civil War. He rode a legendary grey called

Traveller. The horse would outlive his master and lead his funeral procession. Traveller was then himself buried, but not for long. Two years later the army dug up his skeleton and put it in a museum, where Traveller remained on duty until 1902, when he was finally buried.

Old Sorrel, Stonewall Jackson's charger in the Civil War, ended up — standing and stuffed — in the Soldier's Home in Richmond, Virginia.

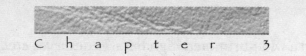

Great Journeys on Horseback

The bond between you and the horse you ride naturally gets stronger with time. What must it be like to spend not a few hours on the same horse, but weeks and months ... and even years?

Tschiffely's Ride

One of the longest journeys ever undertaken on horseback was made by Aime Felix Tschiffely in 1925. His book, *Tschiffely's Ride*, describes in stunning detail his 17,000-kilometre trek from Buenos Aires to New York City with his two Criollo ponies. It took them two and a half years to go the distance.

The Swiss-born Tschiffely, then thirty years old, had been teaching at a school in Argentina, but the notion of a great trek had been in his mind for years. A photograph of him in the book shows an agreeable, freckled man, his arms crossed, his shirt sleeves rolled up past the elbows, and on his head a wide-brimmed high hat. He deserves credit for the journey, but he could never have accomplished it without his two "old pals," Mancha (which means, in Spanish, "the stained one") and Gato ("the cat").

The three could have perished on innumerable occasions. One time, Gato — who was perhaps a little too sure of himself on narrow mountain paths — lost his footing. He was sliding down a mountain and toward certain death when a tree brought him to a halt. Gato had the good sense not to move, but he trembled and neighed pitifully to Mancha while Tschiffely slowly and carefully unsaddled him. With rope and with help, he was able to rescue the pony, but it was a narrow escape.

They nearly drowned in raging rivers. The crossing of canyons on narrow suspension bridges — some of them 150 metres long and only a metre wide — took much courage and a lot of horse sense.

Tschiffely would walk behind Mancha, holding his tail and talking to calm him. When they reached the middle of one sagging and flimsy bridge, it was swaying horribly. Mancha was clever enough to stop until the swaying ceased before proceeding. Had he lost his nerve, bolted or tried to turn back, it would have been the end of them all.

Mancha, sixteen years old when the trek began, had unusual looks: an almost entirely white, piebald face and white stockings, but otherwise quite red. In South America that white face spooked many a horse, most of whom had never seen a face like it. He was as wary as a watchdog, and whenever strangers came near he would lift one leg in warning, flatten his ears and stretch his neck threateningly. When Mancha wanted something from Tschiffely, the pony let him know by nickering or neighing, rubbing his forehead against his master, or nipping him. He would let no one but Tschiffely saddle or ride him, and would buck or kick anyone who tried.

The two ponies were inseparable, but Gato, at fifteen years, was clearly the junior horse in every way. He was a buckskin who never retaliated when Mancha roughed him up. Gato was a willing horse, the kind, Tschiffely wrote, that "if ridden by a brutal man, would gallop until he dropped dead. His eyes had a childish, dreamy look, seeming to observe everything with wondering surprise."

Few ponies could have done what they did — cross deserts without water, navigate dizzying mountain paths and those perilous suspension bridges, penetrate tropical jungles. They were attacked by vampire bats, gnats and mosquitoes. They endured cold mountain winds and steamy jungle heat, and lived on the most meagre fodder. Some of the heartbreakingly steep inclines they climbed were littered with the bleached bones of mules who had died trying to make the ascent. One desert they crossed in Peru was called Matacaballo — Horse-Killer — but even it didn't stop them.

The ancestors of these two Criollo ponies were a blend of Arab and Barb lines. Barbs are the hardy, small horses of north Africa. Criollo ponies had come to Argentina in 1535 with the Spaniards. But when the native people killed the first Spanish settlers, the horses were freed to wander the countryside. Hunted by both humans and wild animals, toughened by cold and heat, drought and hunger, only the strongest survived.

Mancha and Gato were half-wild when Tschiffely bought them, and he thought he was doing them a favour by offering them the finest alfalfa, barley and oats. No thanks, they said, and proceeded to devour the straw given to them as bedding.

The ponies took turns as pack horses, and though Tschiffely picked up the odd fellow traveller along the way, for the most part Mancha and Gato were his only companions. He talked to them a lot, and they seemed to love the sound of his voice. If he said *"Que hay?"* ("What's up?") they would prick their ears and look nervously about. If he said *"puma"* they would sniff the air for lion. They knew that *"chuck-chuck"* meant food, that *"agua"* meant water; they would accelerate to his *"vamos"* and stop at *"bueno."*

Their journey ended in New York, where the mayor welcomed them, and in Washington, where they were greeted by the President of the United States. In New York, while Tschiffely was busy with lectures and public appearances, one well-meaning army sergeant attempted to ride Mancha to give him some exercise. The man later said that the "hellpet" had "gone off like a stick of dynamite."

By now the two ponies and their rider had become true celebrities, and they were put on display at an international horse show in New York. Tschiffely briefly contemplated putting the ponies in a public park in Argentina, but wisely thought better of it. The two ponies got the freedom they deserved.

"As I write these last lines," Tschiffely wrote, "I can see them galloping over the rolling plains until they disappear out of sight in the vastness of the pampas. . . . Good luck to you, old pals, Mancha and Gato."

Across the Plains of Russia

Other men have pulled off some amazing feats of long-distance riding, and so have women. In 1995 a forty-eight-year-old British woman embarked on a six-month-long,

4,200-kilometre journey across the plains of Russia. Barbara Whittome wanted to breed Cossack ponies with her own Arab stock. She had heard that these ponies were the toughest in the world (perhaps she hadn't heard of Mancha and Gato) and decided to test that claim. Besides, she added, "I wasn't in a hurry."

In Volgograd she bought the Cossack ponies and headed east. She took turns riding a palomino stallion named Pompeii, a black mare named Masha, and a grey mare named Malishka. She began the journey with Cossack guides, who were reputed to be tough horsemen. But they complained of saddle sores so much she left them behind and used a compass to guide her instead. A friend followed behind in a truck bearing oats and camping equipment.

Along the way, first Whittome's neighbour Alison, then her own daughter, Katie, joined her. Russian thugs on motorbikes tried to rob their camp, but the mounted women fought them off, and Pompeii even trampled one would-be robber. Barbara's husband later scored it, "Girls on horseback 1, Russian thugs on motorbike 0."

The police stopped them almost daily — but when told of the cross-country pony-trek the officers were so stunned they never examined the women's passports. The weather was fierce in the extreme — from southern Russia's 35°C temperatures to driving sleet in wintry Poland. Barbara's husband expected to encounter at the end a pale, weathered wife. "In fact," he said, "she had never looked better."

"It was the most fantastic experience," Barbara Whittome said. "During the whole trip there was never a moment of regret." She remembers many frustrating incidents but she also remembers the indescribable feeling of freedom that came with crossing the Russian steppes on horseback. She

Barbara Whittome and Pompeii in the snow. (Barbara Whittome)

would do it again — "like a shot" — and is planning more epic rides in Europe and Asia.

The reputation of Cossack riders might have taken a beating on Whittome's trip, but the Cossack ponies had proven their legendary hardiness.

The Long-Distance Riders' Hall of Fame

• Rafael Amador: In 1834 Amador carried an urgent message about a plot to seize land a continent away. Before the telephone, before the telegraph, a man on a horse was still the quickest courier. Amador covered the 4,200 kilometres of jungle, desert, mountain, plain and rivers between Mexico City and Monterey, California in forty-one adventure-filled days.

• Slim John Brown: The scene was right out of an old western movie — American cavalry surrounded by a band of Native warriors — and in true movie-drama style, this man rode for help. He had in his possession some cigarette papers, each stamped with the seal of his superior officer and these words: "Believe the bearer." When his horses died, he used the cigarette papers to "buy" new ones. Brown's wild ride from Los Angeles to San Francisco — 1,000 kilometres — took him four days. The cavalry would be saved.

• Felix X. Aubrey: One historian calls Aubrey the supreme rider of the American West. In 1848 he galloped from Santa Fe, New Mexico to Independence, Missouri in twelve days, setting local tongues wagging. Aubrey then bragged that he could cover the same distance in eight days. He did, but he rode three horses to death, slept only four hours and ate nothing for three days. Finally, Aubrey took bets that he could do the trip in six days — if he used a relay system, Pony Express style. This time he apparently did not stop to eat, sleep or drink. According to one account from the period, Aubrey arrived in Independence "a ghost of a man who could speak only in a hoarse whisper when lifted from his blood-soaked saddle." Still, Aubrey was right on time.

• As Tschiffely had proved, the best long-distance horse is sometimes not a horse at all, but a pony. Then again, sometimes neither horse nor pony wins the marathon ride. To mark 1976, the United States' bicentennial year, the Great American Horse Race took place. It started in Sacramento, California and ended in New York. Each entry was allowed a tiny team (called a remuda) of two mounts, one to ride and one to lead. The race began the last weekend in May and was scheduled to finish on Labour Day in September. Three months and 100 entrants later the winner was a man named Verl Norton — riding a mule!

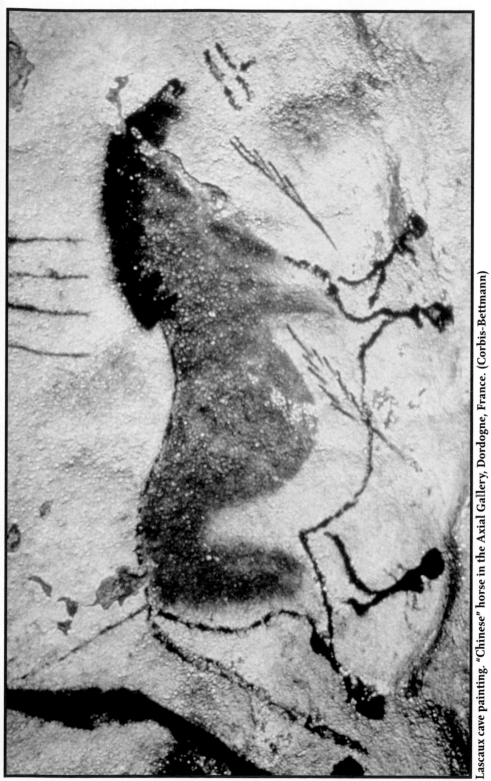

Lascaux cave painting. "Chinese" horse in the Axial Gallery, Dordogne, France. (Corbis-Bettmann)

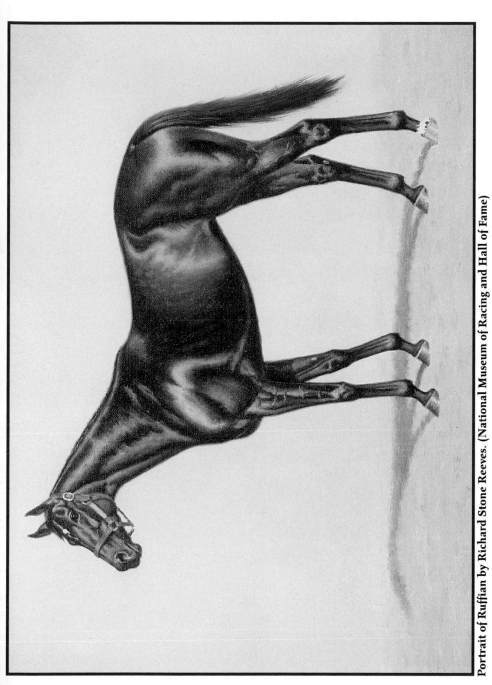

Portrait of Ruffian by Richard Stone Reeves. (National Museum of Racing and Hall of Fame)

Caro Angus and Flag taking the water jump on the cross country course at Checkmate Farms. (CLiX/Shawn Hamilton © 1996)

Nicky can't help hugging her Shetland Pony, Joshua Tree. (CLiX/Shawn Hamilton © 1996)

The "charge" is a highlight of the RCMP's Musical Ride. (RCMP)

It's rare for twins to survive, but brothers Amos and Andy seem to be doing just fine.
(Marilyn Kelley)

Many children's first experience of riding a horse is on a merry-go-round.
(CLiX/Shawn Hamilton © 1996)

Collage of international stamps depicting horses.

Portrait of Secretariat by Jessey R. Turcotte. (National Museum of Racing and Hall of Fame)

Barbara Whittome and Pompeii after their trek across Russia. (B. Whittome)

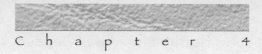
On the Silver Screen and the Printed Page

When a horse gallops or trots, is there a moment when all four hoofs are off the ground?

The hoofs of a fast-moving horse, of course, are too quick for the human eye. One man finally settled the matter in 1872. His ingenious camera work soon inspired moving pictures, and some of the first films ever made, in the 1890s, were about horses. In a way, it is thanks to horses that we have movies.

Now, are all the horse's hoofs ever off the ground at the same time? If you guessed yes, you were right.

We know this thanks to Eadweard Muybridge, who lined up his cameras at a racetrack in California. The process was complicated; like old rifles, old cameras took only single shots. Muybridge connected clocks and circuits and cameras before photographing a celebrated trotter named Occident. The camera shutters would all have to go off in sequence, like a neat row of dominoes falling in rapid succession. And what some photos clearly showed was Occident with all four feet off the ground.

Muybridge continued his studies of the gaits of the horse and other animals. They were eventually collected in a book called *Animals in Motion*. The tiny photos run across the page, comic-book-style. Muybridge also invented a device called the "zoöpraxiscope" to project these images onto a screen. He was soon chatting with Thomas Edison about creating talking pictures by marrying his own zoöpraxiscope and Edison's phonograph.

Someone did just that. Seven years later, Edison made his first film, called *Bucking Bronco*, and then three other short films involving horses: *The Burning Stable*, *Fighting the Fire* and *Elopement on Horseback*.

The silent film had arrived. Then came talking films, then talking films in colour. From the early 1900s until well into the 1950s, horse and cowboy were the stars of thousands of cheaply made movies. People called them "B" movies, and the B may well have stood for "bad." (They were actually movies meant to be the second feature on a double bill — in the days when a single theatre ticket let you see two movies.)

In "B" movies the horse was king — a real character who rescued the hero in the white hat and fooled the bad guys in the black hats. Some movie horses were as famous as the actors. They even got fan mail.

Four-Legged Film Stars

• Fritz, a small red-and-white pinto in films of the 1920s, was ridden by William S. Hart, a fine rider who thought Fritz deserved the same billing he got.

Hart and Fritz jumped through windows and over fire and crossed raging rivers. One film showed Hart riding his

It's easy to see that at some point this horse *does* have all four feet off the ground at once. (John Gierszewki)

horse over a cliff. Movie fans bitterly complained about cruelty to their beloved Fritz. Hart set them straight (he had actually used a fake horse), but the issue of cruelty to horses in Hollywood would come up again.

• Tarzan, a fifty-dollar horse with palomino looks, was portrayed in films of the 1930s as a wonder horse. His sidekick, a cowboy hero named Ken Maynard, was forever getting stuck in quicksand, surrounded by braves or getting knocked unconscious in burning buildings. Tarzan, always, to the rescue!

Tarzan could dance, play dead and untie Maynard's hands. He would even nudge the shy hero into the arms of the heroine for the kiss that always ended the movie.

• Trigger was far and away the most famous movie and TV horse of all time. A palomino ridden by Roy Rogers through the 1940s and 1950s and billed as "the smartest horse in the movies," the 15.2-hand horse was half Thoroughbred and half quarter horse. He could do thirty different tricks, and it was claimed that he appeared in all eighty-seven Roy Rogers movies and in over a hundred of the television shows.

"I have no illusions about my popularity," Roy Rogers once said. "Just as many fans are interested in seeing Trigger as they are in seeing me." Trigger was a merchandiser's dream. In 1949, boys and girls could choose from sixty-five different Roy Rogers/Trigger products, and their comic books were selling at the dizzying rate of two million a month.

Trigger finally died in 1965 at the age of thirty-three. He is remembered for a famous hoofs-in-the-air pose, which you can still see if you go to the Roy Rogers Museum in southern California. Like Comanche, Winchester and the rest, Trigger was mounted for posterity.

Hollywood and Horses

Hollywood and horses have long been partners. In the 1944 film *National Velvet*, for example, Elizabeth Taylor played the role of Velvet Brown. The girl wins a horse in a raffle, disguises herself as a boy and — against all odds — rides the horse to victory in Britain's Grand National Steeplechase. The young Elizabeth Taylor, then only twelve but a rider since the age of four, was determined to get the part. She found out which horse had been chosen for the film and made a point of befriending him.

One scene called for tears as Velvet learns that her sick horse may not live. Another actor advised Taylor that to produce real tears she might imagine her father dying, her brother shoeless, her puppy killed by a car. Elizabeth, who felt no great warmth for her own family but who did love horses, had a better idea: "All I thought about," she said later, "was this horse being very sick, and that I was the little girl who owned him. And the tears came."

Today's actors, much like those of old, sometimes fall in love with their horses. Billy Crystal had never ridden a horse before starring in *City Slickers*, a comedy about a cattle drive. He later bought the horse he rode in that movie. Keifer Sutherland starred in *The Cowboy Way* and later took two years off from acting to compete in rodeos.

Behind the Scenes, a Hard Life for Horses

For the first fifty years of film, children were fed a steady diet of movies that painted the horse as impossibly smart, and above all, devoted to its cowboy pal. In one film from 1912 the hero is tossed off a cliff; his four-legged friend comes by, peeks over the precipice, drops down a rope and hauls him up.

Behind the scenes, though, Hollywood movie directors seemed more concerned about getting action shots than about the safety of animals or riders. In old westerns, for example, the cowboy takes careful aim with his Winchester rifle and in the very next frame a brave and his war pony go down as if felled by an axe. In a way, they were.

Here's how they did it. You drive a post, called a "dead-man," deep into the ground. Attached to it are two lines of thin, strong piano wire (almost impossible to see on film), going from the hoofs of the horse, up the front legs, and back to the girth. This contraption was called "the running W." The stunt man rode the horse at a full gallop and when all the line was played out the horse was suddenly pulled hard to the ground. The dust flew, the rider flew, and the director got the dramatic shot he wanted. But the running W left countless horses dead and many riders disabled for life.

Hollywood got away with this for decades, but the more they made a hero of the horse, the louder the call came to treat the hero kindly. The last straw was a 1949 film called *Jesse James*. The horse who died while making it did not die in vain.

In one scene, the James boys have come to a cliff and the posse is closing in. One brother whacks the flank of his horse, and in the next scene a horse leaps off the cliff and drops into a lake far below. The same shot is then seen again, this time from a different angle, to suggest a second horse leaping. The drop looks to be about thirty metres, and though the next shot shows the James boys and their two horses happily swimming away, not everyone was fooled.

Some movie-goers realized that a horse had died for that shot, and were outraged. That same year the American

Humane Association was formed to monitor the use of animals in movies, and they have been on Hollywood sets ever since to ensure that animals — even insects — are handled with respect. You will often see a note at the end of films today assuring viewers that no animals were treated unkindly in the course of making the film.

The Making of *Black Beauty*

In the 1870s, while Eadweard Muybridge was in California capturing on film the motion of a horse, a very ill but determined woman in Britain was writing a book on horses. The woman's name was Anna Sewell; the book was *Black Beauty*.

When Anna was a girl, a badly sprained ankle left her lame. She got about in a little carriage pulled by a pony. Unlike many coachmen of the time, Anna was kind to the pony and spoke to him as if he understood. She had been influenced by a book that argued for better treatment of all animals. During the last seven years of her life, Anna was confined to a couch. Here she would write, when able, what she referred to as her "little book" on the life of a horse called Black Beauty. (The horse might have been based on Anna's brother's horse, a mare called Bessie who possessed great spirit, good sense and unusual quickness.)

The narrator of the story is Black Beauty himself — distinguished by his glossy black coat, his one white foot and "the pretty white star" on his forehead. Horses in the book speak to each other and share their life stories. No one had written a book in the voice of a horse before, and the effect was just as Anna intended — "to induce kindness, sympathy, and an understanding treatment of horses."

Anna Sewell could not have imagined that Beauty would

45

BLACK
BEAUTY

ANNA SEWELL

Illustrated by
DINAH DRYHURST

The touching story of Black Beauty has made the book a best seller, and inspired new editions like this fully-illustrated version by Dinah Dryhurst. (Courtesy of Breslich & Foss)

live on in the hearts of young readers as he has. *Black Beauty* is reputedly the sixth-best-selling book of all time.

* * *

For whatever reason, girls usually discover horses before boys do. At riding stables all across Canada, girls far out-number boys. And it's likely no coincidence that many of the horse novels for young readers have been written by women.

Anna Sewell's *Black Beauty* may still be read centuries from now. The same may hold true for Marguerite Henry's *Misty of Chincoteague*, *King of the Wind* and *Black Gold*. Mary O'Hara, who wrote *My Friend Flicka* and others in that series, is in the same category. These books still have a lot to teach us about the bond between horses and children.

Boys and men warm to horses as well, of course. C.S. Lewis's classic Narnia chronicles feature plenty of talking horses. And the Black Stallion series was written by Walter Farley, a city boy whose uncle — a professional horseman — taught him to know and love horses. He wrote the first of the series when he was still a very young man, and would go on to write twenty more. *The Black Stallion*, published in 1941, opens with a boy and a sleek black stallion on a steamship. Alec leaves lumps of sugar on the fierce horse's stall window and is later rewarded for his kindness when both are ship-wrecked on an island off the Spanish coast.

My Friend Flicka, also published in 1941, reminds us that gentling (introducing the horse non-violently to bridle, sad-dle and rider) has a long history. In a way, Flicka seems ahead of its time. If gentling has become fashionable, maybe this story about a boy and his horse can take some small credit for the change.

The boy's father Rob, for example, is a hard-nosed ranch-er, but he hates bronco-busting, the often brutal "breaking" of a horse: "It ruins a horse! . . . He loses something and never gets it back."

Rob's ideal horse trainer is his wife Nell. Like modern-day gentlers, she approaches the trembling horse slowly and patiently. She lets the horse smell her, and then turns her back to the horse. When the horse nuzzles her back, Nell turns and begins talking to the horse, stroking her. Only when the horse shows no fear does she rise into the saddle and begin the work.

Heed every sign, Rob McLaughlin tells young Ken about the ways of horses — "the way it moves its body, the ears, the eyes; the little whinnies — that's its way of talking . . ." Once you learn its language and it learns yours, the father says, friendship with an animal becomes something special.

* * *

For some kids who can't get enough horsey material, movies about horses and books about horses are just the beginning. Some girls convert their rooms into shrines to horses and ponies. Horse show ribbons line the top of their bunk beds, figurines of horses and ponies form little herds on tables. Horse posters, horse calendars, horse mugs and plates hold pride of place in the room, near the neatly parked saddle, riding helmet and crop.

The smell of horse leather in the room, the horse books and videos on the shelves, the little silhouette of the horse on the lamp announce to one and all: here lives a member of the club.

The girls grow up to be women, but sometimes the horse fever still rages and their places still look ruled by the horse. One lovely autumn day I rode down some back roads in Vermont with friends, most of them women with sons and daughters of their own. Every woman's living room, I later

Some girls' rooms have become shrines to horses, with everything from figurines to posters to ribbons! (Sandra Bogart Johnston)

noticed, was awash with horse photographs, paintings, sculptures. One woman offered us coffee around a splendid wooden table whose centrepiece was a carved oaken animal. A horse, of course.

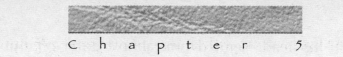

Sport Horse Heroes

Ruffian

Her name was Ruffian — a big black filly with striking good looks. Walter Farley eyed her and said she was the horse he had in mind as he wrote the Black Stallion books. One race veterinarian called her the most perfectly conformed — best balanced and proportioned — horse he had ever seen. She was a beauty, with twin gifts of spirit and speed. Thoroughbred racing is dominated by colts, but this filly would be an exception. Some say she was not just the greatest filly, but the greatest racehorse, who ever lived.

The man who first rode her on the track was astonished by her long fluid stride. Former jockey Yates Kennedy, then fifty-nine, had been around horses all his life, and Ruffian's ride was so effortless he thought he had gone the three-eighths-of-a-mile distance in thirty-seven seconds, maybe a fraction more.

Like many jockeys and show jumpers, he had a little stopwatch in his head. Kennedy was almost never off, but this day he was — by a full two seconds. He later said it was as if the horse had put up a sail between strides, and that while off the ground she rode the wind at her back.

Ruffian was born in April, 1972 at Claiborne Farm, one of the grand old breeding farms of Kentucky. Her owners had picked the name Ruffian for a certain colt, and when he was sold they gave the name to this little filly. "Girls," said her owner, Barbara Janney, "can be Ruffians too." And she didn't become a delicate little mare. Stablehands nicknamed her Sophie, as in sofa. As in big as a couch. But she was not big and awkward, she was big and graceful.

Before that first day when trainer Frank Y. Whiteley put the jockey on Ruffian for her initial training ride, he defied a superstition at the track: he sang her praises. So much in racing depends on luck — drawing your starting position from a hat, breaking too soon or too late and losing a race by a fraction of a second, the mood of the horse, the footing, the weather. . . . Wise track people never sing a horse's praises before praise has been properly earned. Best not anger the god of luck. But old Whiteley was sure that Ruffian's star would shine a long time, for the gods themselves had given her something special.

"I got a big black filly I'm gonna put you on," he told the rider. "It's the fastest horse you've ever been on."

In a short race against other horses at the stable, the jockey, Jacinto Vasquez, kept a tight hold on Ruffian, but she breezed by the others. With this horse, the trick was not to find the gas pedal, but the brakes. It took every ounce of Jacinto's considerable strength to stop her from continuing to run when the race ended. His hands and arms went numb from pulling. Old Whiteley was right. He had never ridden a horse like Ruffian.

In her first race, on May 22, 1974, against other untried fillies, she opened up a fifteen-length lead and matched the track record. This would be her pattern. Though fate would cut short her career, in nine of her ten races she either matched or broke the track record — sometimes a record that had stood for decades. In the tenth, the jockey was specifically instructed to coast to victory and not to break any records.

Ruffian won her second race by seven lengths, her third by thirteen lengths! Racing magazines called her "a wonder." They said she was "invincible." Still, she had never run against a colt.

How fast, went the whisper, can she run?

Someone had an idea. Run Ruffian against the best colt of the day — Kentucky Derby winner Foolish Pleasure. Just those two horses. The Great Match Race would be held July 6, 1975. Boy versus Girl. Him versus Her. The Race of the Century.

People wore buttons to the race, and some of the 50,000 spectators at Belmont that day seemed to divide along gender lines. Men and boys wore Foolish Pleasure buttons. Women and girls showed their support for Ruffian by wearing her button. One newspaper ran a cartoon showing women known for their outspoken views on women's rights all yelling "C'mon Ruffian!"

In most races, colts will outrun mares. They're bigger, stronger, and sometimes they intimidate fillies. But many experts were picking Ruffian in this rare match race. She was the bigger horse — taller by almost two hands, heavier by almost thirty kilograms.

Barbara Janney would always remember a particular

moment when Ruffian halted briefly as she was being led past the grandstand prior to the race. The crowd was roaring — and this was *before* the race. Ruffian paused to consider these onlookers, as if certain that she was the centre of all this attention. Janney would savour that memory because of what followed. Maybe that's how she wanted to remember Ruffian, composed and self-assured, aware of her own greatness.

When the gates broke open, Foolish Pleasure smartly took the lead on the outside, but in several strides Ruffian nosed out in front on the inside. She was so much bigger than he was that fans in the stands could not see the colt as the two horses rounded the turn. The filly looked to be running alone.

Near the halfway point it happened. Both jockeys heard a sharp snap. It's the sound a branch makes when it comes down in a storm. It's the sound a horse's leg makes when it fractures, a sound that those who have heard it never forget, or want to hear again.

Ruffian had broken her left front leg, had taken what the Thoroughbred world calls "a bad step." It's an almost light-hearted phrase that appears to blame the horse for a numbing, life-ending event.

The hoof, suddenly loose and flapping, no longer supported that front leg. She was running on raw bone — which splintered, one vet said later, like an ice cube hit with a hammer.

At the moment the leg broke, Ruffian appeared to bump Foolish Pleasure. But the videotapes reveal that she was *leaning* on him, trying to compensate, trying to stay up and keep running. On she ran, impossibly it now seems, for fifty more metres. Then she veered right and staggered to a halt. The jockey leapt off and tried to support Ruffian, who screamed in pain.

In the stands there was disbelief and utter silence. Even the race announcer paused, as if he too could not comprehend. Some in the crowd began to weep: women and girls wearing T-shirts emblazoned with the name Ruffian and the circle-and-cross symbol of womanhood; men and boys who had a moment before cheered Foolish Pleasure's apparent burst of speed.

By gamely continuing to run Ruffian had made the injury many times worse. She thrashed and threw off the temporary cast they put on her, along with another following surgery. She came out of the anaesthesia and tried to run — maybe from the pain or to catch Foolish Pleasure, maybe because every other bone in her body told her to. "The same thing that made her win," said her vet, "made her die."

Finally, the distraught Barbara Janney asked that the suffering cease. In a rare and private ceremony at Belmont the next evening, they buried Ruffian. She was bound in white like a mummy, and a great hydraulic lift gently laid her in her grave, her head pointing toward the finish line. Looking on were the grief-stricken Whiteley, exercise riders and stable hands, and Jacinto Vasquez in a dark suit. One of them laid on Ruffian two blankets she had worn, then the machines covered her with earth, and a great horseshoe wreath was set atop her grave.

There is a stone marker there now, listing Ruffian's victories. And sometimes people send flowers to Belmont and ask that they be placed by the obelisk. The senders no doubt remember, with sadness and with joy, how the beautiful black filly put up sails between strides and rode the wind.

Canada's Pride, Northern Dancer

If ever a horse was a gold mine, it was the colt named Northern Dancer — the greatest racehorse Canada has ever produced. On rare occasions, foals in the paddock don't follow the mare. It is the foal who leads, the mare who follows. Northern Dancer was like that — born with presence.

Like a pilgrim drawn to the shrine, I have been to stall number two in the green foaling barn at Windfields Farm, just northeast of Toronto, where Northern Dancer was born. He was a bay, with black mane and tail, three white stockings and a thick blaze that ran from his forelock down into one nostril.

The farm put him up for sale, and one buyer did take him home for a closer look, but brought him back. Too little, too chunky, too feisty. Having, and then returning, Northern Dancer is like holding in your hands a winning lottery ticket, and then losing it. Buyers in France later offered $40 million for this horse. Before he died in 1990, Northern Dancer had sired 1,000 foals, commanding up to $1 million for each one.

He had his own style of running, not the long easy stride of Ruffian, but a choppy gallop. A magnificent photograph, taken at the rail of Churchill Downs the day he won the Kentucky Derby in 1964, shows him kicking up more turf than any other horse in view. His time in the Derby was a scorching two minutes flat, a new record. Only Secretariat would do better — by a mere three-fifths of a second. As old-timers at the track sometimes say, "He ran a hole in the wind."

But it was as a breeding stallion that Northern Dancer really left his mark. Bernard McCormack, the Irish-born manager at Windfields, said that "the story of Northern

Northern Dancer after winning the Preakness in 1964, on his way to the Belmont Stakes to try for the Triple Crown. (UPI/Corbis-Bettmann)

Dancer is a story without an end because it's still being written." His bloodline may well create more champions than that of any horse who ever lived.

Naturally, all forgave him his princely bearing. "He had an ego," says McCormack, "the size of Mount Everest. He would pose for the cameras and would not come in from the paddock until he decided it was his time. He would make you wait; you wouldn't go out to the field to bring him in because he'd run you over. But he was Northern Dancer and you make allowances for a horse like that."

Secretariat: The Horse with Heart

When Secretariat died, the chestnut stallion's body was taken to the University of Kentucky where a veterinary surgeon performed the autopsy.

"We were all shocked," he said afterwards. The doctor had seen or performed thousands of autopsies on horses, but nothing prepared him for the sight of Secretariat's heart. It was almost twice normal size, and one-third bigger than any equine heart he had ever seen. "And it wasn't pathologically enlarged," said the surgeon. "All the chambers and the valves were normal. It was just larger. I think it told us why he was able to do what he did."

When Secretariat won the Kentucky Derby in 1973, he came from dead last and went faster in each successive quarter-mile. He then came first in the Preakness before winning the Belmont by thirty-one lengths, and, by winning those three races, captured the prestigious Triple Crown of Thoroughbred racing. Secretariat did not toy with the opposition; there was no opposition.

What endeared Secretariat to millions of people was not just his blinding speed, but his gentle spirit and his playfulness. His jockey, Ron Turcotte, often went to the farm to see Secretariat in retirement, and he was certain the horse recognized him. The horse would trot across the paddock, stop at the fence in front of Turcotte and stick his tongue out. Turcotte would take the horse's tongue in his hand, shake it and say Hello. When that greeting was over, the horse would rub his face against his old jockey.

Turcotte fondly remembers the horse's great intelligence and looks, what a ham he was for photographers, how willing and generous in a race, how powerful and yet how kind. He was a horse who loved humans, and was, in Turcotte's words, "as sweet as a lamb."

Every year 10,000 people would visit Claiborne Farm in Kentucky to pay homage to Secretariat. But by the fall of 1989, the horse had laminitis, a life-threatening hoof disease. One morning his groom rose at dawn to check on the failing horse. Secretariat lifted his head and nickered loudly — "like he was beggin' me for help," the groom would later say. At 11:45 one October morning, they put him down. The big heart would beat no more.

The Horse Called Halla

One of my favourite horse stories concerns a German show-jumping rider named Hans Winkler and his extremely clever horse, a tall bay mare named Halla. Until Winkler worked with her, she had a reputation as a difficult and nervous horse.

They were riding in a show-jumping event at the 1956 Olympic Games in Stockholm, Sweden, when Winkler pulled a groin muscle. Despite the pain, he urged Halla to take the last fence, which she did.

But now they were in the jump-off. Winkler would have

to ride again, despite his injury. Still in terrible pain, he had to be lifted up into the saddle. Some people thought it was madness to face huge fences on a high-strung mare when the rider could do little more than point the horse at the jumps.

An astute writer and trainer named Vicki Hearne later applauded both Winkler's trust in his horse and the horse's great achievement. "Imagine a race-car driver," she wrote, "suddenly unable to operate clutch, brake and accelerator except in a distant, awkward and weak fashion."

In show jumping the takeoff point is critical. If the horse leaps too soon or too late, if the horse loses focus for an instant, the rail comes down. Horses too fast or too slow will not manage a jump-off course. Turns can be neither too tight nor too wide. Call it a game of chess played at high speed.

But the rider, not the horse, calls the shots. The rider's mind is racing between the riding itself, the sequence of jumps and number of strides between them, the seconds allowed. But when Winkler rode Halla that day, all he could do was vaguely hope the horse would do it all herself.

And she did. Halla won an individual gold medal for Winkler, and team gold for Germany. When Winkler was helped out of the saddle, he did the right thing: he threw his arms around Halla and thanked her.

Moifaa: The Long Shot

The story of this steeplechaser at the turn of the century reads like the plot of a Walt Disney film.

Bred in New Zealand, Moifaa was a clumsy, odd-looking horse, a huge brown gelding more than seventeen hands tall. Some thought him ugly and claimed he had the head and shoulders of a camel. "It was impossible not to notice him, with his giant head and high withers," wrote steeplechase historian Anne Holland. "Everything about him was big."

He was thought to have only a slim chance in the 1904 British Grand National — at four and a half miles (over seven kilometres) long, and with thirty jumps, the most famous and gruelling steeplechase event in the world. Few horses even finish the race. But Moifaa had won nine of thirteen races at home, and so his trainer, Spencer Gollan, decided to ship him the 25,000 kilometres from New Zealand to England eight months before the Grand National.

Moifaa's custom-built stall was placed up on the deck of the ship. But off the coast of Ireland the ship encountered a storm and finally broke in half. Moifaa would have drowned had he not used his hoofs to kick the stall to pieces. The horse managed to stay afloat despite seven- to ten-metre-high waves, and eventually made his way to an island, where he lived on marsh grass. (Strangely enough, Moifaa's father was a horse called Natator, which means "the swimmer.") One day a lone fisherman saw him parading angrily up and down a sandbar a kilometre from shore.

When the horse was captured and taken to the nearest port, someone recognized him as Moifaa, long thought to be drowned. A photograph of Spencer Gollan shows a man with a handlebar moustache and kind eyes; he welcomed Moifaa at the docks with lumps of sugar. But even he had to admit that this drawn horse had little chance in the upcoming Grand National. The bookies agreed. Moifaa was ranked a 25-to-1 long shot.

But win it he did, over twenty-five other horses. Not only that, Moifaa crossed the finish line eight lengths ahead of the nearest horse!

Eclipse First, and the Rest Nowhere

No listing of great horses, even a brief one, would be complete without mentioning Eclipse, the magnificent chestnut who never lost a race. Almost seventeen hands high, he was unusual in his conformation, with hindquarters slightly higher than his withers, and with a long slim neck.

Eclipse won at least eighteen races, and before he died in 1789 sired the greatest line of winners the world has ever seen. In 1979 someone calculated that of the horses who had won 170 major races that year around the world, eighty-two percent could be traced back to Eclipse! (Only time will tell whether that other great sire, Northern Dancer, will ultimately "eclipse" Eclipse's record.)

Born during an eclipse of the sun, the colt was originally owned by a duke. The sheep farmer who later bought him found he could not handle the horse. At the age of five he was leased to an Irish-born army captain named Denis O'Kelly. His first race was at Epsom, where he easily won the first of his two four-mile (six-and-a-half-kilometre) heats.

O'Kelly went to a local inn and there bragged that he could predict the order of finish for the next day's race. Someone called his bluff, so he wrote on a piece of paper his prediction, with instructions that it be read aloud after the race. When Eclipse won next day by a quarter of a mile, O'Kelly's note took on the feel of prophecy. Etched forever into the lore of racing history were his words: "Eclipse first, and the rest nowhere."

Arkle of Ireland

The Irish have a special feel for the horse, and the fine rains that fall on that land's fertile soil make for almost perfect pastures, and, sometimes, almost perfect horses. Arkle was one.

He may well have been the greatest steeplechaser of all time. He was born in County Dublin in 1957 — a stringy bay with black mane and tail, large eyes and almost mulish ears.

Arkle was a natural jumper who, some bragged, could leap the mountain in Scotland that was his namesake. Brave and determined as a racer, he was also an unusually sociable horse who loved visitors (he would nose around their pockets for treats), was kind to children, and was even friendly to dogs. His favourite meal, served at 4:30 every afternoon, consisted of mash mixed with six fresh eggs, oats and that crowning touch — two bottles of black Irish beer.

But for all his playfulness in the paddock, on the racecourse he was unmatched — he won twenty-five races, including three consecutive Cheltenham Gold Cups. So badly did he beat other horses (sometimes by thirty lengths), that some started to call him a "killer" horse when other horses died trying to catch him. In his last race, in 1966, the great Irish horse hit a guard rail and cracked a bone in his foot. It must have caused him great pain to run. But run he did. When Arkle finished a close second, many in the stands that day wept to see him limp back to the unsaddling ring.

"We will never," said his jockey, Pat Taaffe, "see his likes again."

Niatross and the Race Against the Clock

When this speedy American trotter with the star in the middle of his forehead went on a farewell tour of nine North American tracks in 1996, he drew up to 18,000 admirers. They came to pat his nose, to take his photograph, to stand in awe. For Niatross was truly a wonder.

In a two-year career of thirty-nine races, the tall dark bay won thirty-seven of them. By 1979 he was valued at $10 million and was already being called the standard-bred horse of the century. But as with Ruffian, the whisper followed him: How fast can Niatross go? No other horse could keep up with him, so it was decided that the stallion would race time itself. The aim was to break the record set by another horse, Steady Star, in 1971.

On October 1, 1980, at Lexington, Kentucky, Niatross would challenge the world-record time of 1 minute 52 seconds for the mile (over one and a half kilometres). Two Thoroughbreds, galloping alongside and pulling carts, would simulate race conditions. But it was really Niatross versus the clock.

Other great trotters had shaved fractions of seconds off the world record in time trials. With driver Clint Galbraith in the sulky behind, Niatross slashed a full three seconds from the mark. Had he actually raced former record holder Steady Star, he would have won by a staggering fourteen lengths.

The Mystery of Phar Lap

The Red Terror. Red Lightning. Big Red. All names for Phar Lap, a name that means, in Thai, lightning or "wink of the sky." Phar Lap was a seventeen-hand chestnut horse you could put a toddler on, but who would buck experienced jockeys who dared tell him what to do.

He was a brilliant horse with a great sense of mischief. He would grab grooms by the shirt, tug sharply and whinny gleefully when the shirt ripped. Phar Lap adored his personal groom, Tommy Woodcock, who always had a cube of sugar for him and called him Bobby Boy. In fact, the two became so close that Phar Lap would often refuse to eat unless Tommy was there in the stall along with him.

In the late 1920s and early 1930s, he won thirty-six races in three years and was so popular that his trainer's wife once remarked, "He's not our horse. I think every child in Australia owns him."

But Phar Lap's success had a price. People lost large sums of money betting against him, and at one point a gunman reportedly tried to shoot him. Tommy Woodcock, desperate to save his friend, deliberately put himself and a pony in the line of fire to keep his beloved Bobby from being hurt.

Phar Lap died in California, suddenly and mysteriously, in Tommy's arms. Some say he was poisoned. Like Secretariat, he had great heart in every way.

Man O'War

They called him Big Red around the barn, and everything about Man O'War was big. His appetite. His size. His reputation.

Born March 29, 1917 at the height of the First World War (and thus his name), Man O'War quickly became a national hero in the United States, where extraordinary offers were made to buy him. One Hollywood movie producer dangled a million dollars in front of Man O'War's owner; a Texas cattle baron and oilman named W.T. Waggoner simply signed a blank cheque and invited the horse's owner to name his price. But Man O'War was not for sale.

He seemed to inspire a huge affection in everyone who saw him run. His workout times were often faster than his race times, which were themselves extraordinary. Man O'War ran for the pure joy of it, quickly staking out his position at the front and defying any horse to catch him or even to get close.

He lost only one race: a poor start left him ten lengths behind but he easily made that up and could have won had he not been boxed in along the rail. The winning horse that day was called, fittingly, Upset, and his jockey, Willie Knapp, later wished he had just moved over and let the great horse breeze past. "So great a champion as Man O'War," he said with respect and great feeling, "deserved to retire undefeated."

He was the kind of horse no owner wanted to race against. Man O'War won one of his twenty-one races by 100 lengths, and when he set record times it was not by a fraction of a second but six seconds or more! He set three world records, two American records and three track records — all effortlessly. Save for that one loss, he was never pressed.

Man O'War was imposing in every way: at 16.4 hands, the glowing red chestnut had a huge stride and emperor's manners. All his life he fussed about being saddled. And yet he was playful too: like an obedient dog, he would carry in his mouth his groom's hat. For all his racing career, his stable mate was a gentle old hunter named Major Treat.

Man O'War's two favourite things? To run and to eat. So huge was his appetite that his handlers sometimes kept a bit in his mouth to stop him from wolfing down his food. Every day Man O'War consumed all the hay he could eat, almost five kilograms of oats and a handful of carrots. As a racer, he weighed a hefty 523 kilograms and by the time he became a breeding stallion he shot up to 623 kilograms.

A track writer of the day, Joe Palmer, remembers how — even standing in his stall — "energy still poured from him. He could get in no position which suggested actual repose, and his very stillness was that of the coiled spring, and of the crouched tiger."

The statue of Man O'War attracts thousands of visitors every year to the Kentucky Horse Park. (Karen Briggs)

Even as a stately twenty-five-year-old, Man O'War never stopped thinking he was a champion. They had to lock him in his stall to prevent him from challenging young stallions in adjacent pastures. Come on, he would say, race me. And that's how he will be remembered: mane flying, tail high and proud, the stride long and easy.

Beloved "Freaks"

Many of the horses who ran to greatness are described as odd in some way — a head too big, a neck too slim, withers too high, a disposition too fiery. Few of these horses look or act "normal." Great horses, trainers say, are "freaks." Trainers use the term with real affection to describe horses whose physical gifts, courage and intelligence combine to let that horse do what he does so well.

Big Ben, twice world champion in the show-jumping ring in the late 1980s, was called a freak. He has a short neck and a big head, and he makes such an odd noise in his throat when he lands that it put off many would-be buyers. But this oddity of a horse, first sold for just $2,000, was eventually ridden by Ian Millar in three Olympic Games. At Spruce Meadows in Calgary, he twice won the Masters — the richest and most hotly contested show-jumping prize in the world. Big Ben also won the Derby there, a true test of courage and stamina, six times! It's a safe bet that that record will never be matched. The odds are also against another horse winning the world championship, not just twice, but two years in a row. Big Ben was in a league of his own.

Canada's equestrian hero, the high-jumping, muffin-loving Big Ben. (Jayne Huddleston)

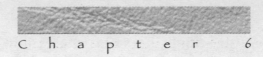

True Tales and Tall Tales

Summer. Riding in the paddock. There are beads of sweat across your forehead where your riding helmet or cowboy hat meets your hairline. You and others later gather round your instructor's kitchen table for a cool glass of juice. . . . Talk turns, as it always does, to horses.

Trading horse stories is like trading coins. We offer them as proof — of horse character, stubbornness, intelligence (or lack of it), courage, devotion or high spirit. The stories say to those who prize horses, See? I told you so.

Morocco

One of the most enduring clever horse stories concerns a six-teenth-century horse in England called Morocco. Shake-speare's play *Love's Labour's Lost* refers to "the dancing horse" — this was Morocco.

A medium-sized bay with a docked tail, he was owned and trained by a Scotsman named Thomas Banks. Morocco could dance a jig, climb the spiral staircase of a London cathedral, and walk on his hind legs (forward, backward and in circles). It seemed he could also count. Someone would throw dice and Morocco would tap out the number that came up. Shown the glove of someone in the audience, Morocco could even pick out its owner.

Clearly, Thomas Banks must have been passing sly signs to his horse. Credit Morocco for his attentiveness, credit Banks for his showmanship. But perhaps they were too clever. The sixteenth century was obsessed with magic and witchcraft, and there were severe penalties for practising either.

Unable to understand such a gifted horse and trainer, audiences concluded it was the work of a sorcerer. Banks once ducked prison by having the horse kneel before a man wearing a crucifix in his hat; Morocco then rose and kissed the cross. Here was proof, and just in the nick of time, of the horse's holiness.

But in Rome, the pope denounced both man and horse as devil worshippers. Banks either escaped or was pardoned, because he did live to a ripe old age. Some say he went into the wine business. Of Morocco nothing was heard again.

About a century later the public reacquired a taste for trick ponies. In 1770 a former sergeant-major in the British cavalry, Philip Astley, launched the first equestrian circus in London, a show that led to others in Dublin and Paris. His amphitheatres were circular arenas with magnificent chandeliers and four tiers of seating. They looked like opera houses, with horses, not singers, at the centre.

Astley's horses could dance a minuet, lie down on command and play dead during mock battles, not stirring until asked. Most famous of all was Billy, The Little Learned

Military Horse. Like Morocco, he could count (taking his cue from the clicking of his master's fingernails, as perhaps Morocco had done). Billy could spell Astley's name in the earth with his hoof, distinguish gold from silver and ladies from gentlemen, and pluck a handkerchief from its owner's pocket. Even in old age, Billy would, on command, wash his feet in water, remove his own saddle, or lift a boiling kettle from a fire.

How Clever Was Clever Hans?

A century later, along came a cart horse in Germany known as Clever Hans. His story is still used by scientists to correct false notions of animal intelligence. Clever Hans, these professors insist, was not so clever at all. (Or were they just attempting to show how smart humans are by showing that animals aren't?)

Hans's owner was Herr Wilhelm von Osten, a Prussian nobleman who was impressed by how cleverly a particular horse backed a cart along a circular driveway. (Try hooking up a wagon to your bicycle and then backing up in a circle and you will see how devilishly difficult it is.) An eccentric, von Austen thought he could teach Hans to think. He taught the horse to respond to questions, either by tapping his hoofs a certain number of times to respond to a mathematical question, or by selecting the correct wooden alphabet block. Word spread. Clever Hans became world famous.

Was Hans a thinking horse? Or another Morocco? The world wanted to know. So on September 6, 1904, a committee of thirteen people — including a zoologist, a veterinarian and a psychologist — set out to determine the answer.

The panel was both amazed and stumped. They were

convinced that Hans was not actually doing the math. ("Let's see, two buckets of oats plus two buckets of oats equals, um, four buckets of oats.") But if the horse was reading signs from von Osten, what signs?

Finally someone proved that the horse was reading the body language of the questioner. When von Osten asked his questions out of sight, the horse was lost for an answer. Clever Hans — perhaps by observing his master's eyes or eyebrows, or rate of breathing, or a slight flaring of the nostrils — caught the clue. But he had to have his questioner in full view.

The world of science seemed pleased: a "dumb" animal had been restored to its rightful place below humankind. Even von Osten, who never meant to cue the horse, felt Hans had let him down. He died soon afterward, a bitter and disillusioned man.

But the question remains: Why did Clever Hans not receive more credit for his ability to read signs so subtle that thirteen learned observers could not easily detect them? Today we know a lot more about animals, and perhaps the more we learn, the less arrogant we will be.

Gentle Giants

In the late 1940s the Union Milk Company in Calgary still delivered milk by horse-drawn wagon. A new horse — likely a massive Percheron or Belgian, with furry feet the size of pie plates — had been given a route near the dairy so he could learn the ropes. At one point the driver ducked into a house to make a delivery, and when he returned he clucked to the horse: Let's go.

The horse refused. Three times the driver slapped the horse on the back with the reins. The horse stood statue-still.

Draft horses like this Belgian mare and foal are huge! (John Gierszewski)

Finally, the driver got out to investigate. Clutching the legs of the horse was a three-year-old boy. The horse had not only tolerated this, but apparently out of concern for the boy's safety, had refused to move. This is a story about the horse as guardian angel.

Then there are stories about the horse as creature of habit. The ancient Greeks loved to race horses, as we do. A mare called Aura threw her jockey early in an Olympic race, but galloped on — just as horses in steeplechase races will often continue round the course, even when the jockey is eight ditches back in a heap. But this horse went a step further: she did precisely the required number of loops around the track, beat all the other horses, then stopped in front of the judge's stand. To receive her prize, of course.

Humans as Honorary Horses

Some horse stories flatter *us*. These are stories of horses displaying affection, even devotion, to their riders.

Lucy Rees, author of *The Horse's Mind*, has coined a phrase to describe the bond between rider and horse. She believes that when you gain the trust of a horse, he lets you into his society — equine society. You become what Rees calls "an honorary horse."

Maybe this story concerns a horse and an honorary one. The woman who tells it offers it as proof of the protectiveness of horses, or at least of one horse in particular. The woman was in a corral with two horses when she suddenly had a dizzy spell and collapsed. One horse panicked and circled in a frenzy. At that point the woman lost consciousness. When she awoke, she was flat on her back and staring up, not into blue sky, but into the massive belly of the other horse, a Clydesdale mare.

The mare had created for the woman the only safe place in the corral. The mare's body and eyes kept the other, nervous horse at bay. When the woman finally felt strong enough to rise, the mare lowered her neck, which the woman used to help pull herself up.

Sticking with Dr. Broom

The horse-fevered are naturally drawn to such tales of horse generosity. Anne Zander, for example, rides a horse named Dr. Broom, a 16.3-hand Thoroughbred with impressive bloodlines. He had never raced because — true to his ornery temperament — he refused to leave the starting gate. "All red-head with an attitude" was how Anne described him. The horse regularly kicked and bit, stepped on, lashed at, and ran away with his rider.

While haying one year, Anne injured her back and required surgery. She lay abed for weeks, imagining Dr. Broom in his stall — a wind-up alarm clock wound tighter and tighter and set to go off with a bang. When she finally got out of the hospital, her back still ached and her left leg felt useless. Still, she was determined to ride. And how did Dr. Broom react to his essentially disabled rider?

"My wild horse," says Anne, "was a perfect gentleman. He stood stock-still for me to haul myself on. He did not move until I asked. I had no balance and had to hang on to his mane. If I started to lose my balance, or the pain was intolerable, I just said 'whoa' and he would stop. We tried a few trot steps and a few at canter. He was a letter-perfect Pony Club horse."

Later, Anne's coach got on. "Doc" promptly tried to buck him. Anne is left amazed by all this, and grateful. "He can still be a red-hot chestnut, but he came through for me at a time when I needed him most."

A Risky Business

Some horse people tend to be forgiving of even nasty horses. If the horse is mean, a rider or trainer made him that way. The notion of horses born with a killer instinct is not one that many who love horses want to consider. But whether born or made, mean-spirited horses do exist. The power of horses is part of their attraction, but falls and kicks and misadventure can take a dreadful toll on riders.

Sometimes pure luck, the bad kind, can change a rider's life.

Christopher Reeve, an actor remembered for his role in the Superman movies, fell from a horse in 1995. Barring some medical advance, he will spend the rest of his days in a wheelchair. Every year in the United States, some 50,000 people are injured riding horses, and 200 die. But a reporter went around to the New York stable where Reeve fell and asked the riders: Has the accident given you pause? The answer, invariably, was no.

Making Sense of Horse Sense

Horse sense is a mysterious thing. Sometimes it saves lives. Years ago a cart horse in Spain stubbornly refused to enter a mountain tunnel she had passed through countless times before. Traffic backed up behind her, and one can imagine the stern tactics employed to move her. Still, the horse would not move. When the tunnel collapsed shortly afterwards, the mare was hailed as a hero.

Why did horses in San Francisco thrash around and break free of their stalls hours before an earthquake struck on April 18, 1906? How to explain the many documented stories of horses getting their riders safely home through unfamiliar jungles and in winter white-outs?

Call it horse sense. But we might also be on the lookout for horse manure. During the Mexican Revolution, a general's palomino named Canelo could supposedly smell rebel soldiers twenty-four kilometres away. Because of the horse's "talent" he was allowed to graze unhobbled around the camp. He would sense the enemy and then, good bodyguard that he was, awaken the general by nipping him and pawing the ground.

One night, the general was inside a house. (It must have been a very large house, for it also housed Canelo and the army.) At two in the morning the horse began to whinny, and finally kicked the door open. The general got the message; he and his men saddled up and waited on a nearby hilltop. Some 600 rebels were killed in the ensuing ambush.

Equally strange is the story of Fred Kimball, a horse psychic used by some of the top-ranked horse trainers and riders in North America. A sailor all his life, he had — he claimed — mastered the art of mind-reading. Until he died in 1996 at the age of ninety-two, riders would give Fred a call at his home in California, tell him the horse's name and age, and Fred would diagnose the horse's psychological or physical ailment. For twenty-five dollars. He would trust you to pop a cheque in the mail.

One time a horse bucked a rider at an eventing competition in Orillia, Ontario and galloped away. All attempts at finding him failed. Call Fred, someone suggested, after the horse had been missing for three days. Fred described a particular valley by water and said the horse was suffering with a shoulder problem. A local person identified the place, and there was the missing horse — sore shoulder and all.

Mascots

Some horses, especially race horses, are nervous in their stalls and need little "mascots" to calm them and keep them company. Exterminator, a Kentucky Derby winner, grew attached to a Shetland pony named Peanuts. Over the course of twenty-one years, he had three pony friends, loved them all, and mourned them when they died.

A famous racehorse of the eighteenth century, called the Darley Arabian, was befriended by a cat who used to sit on his back in the stable or nestle close to him. When the horse died, his old pal refused to eat, and finally died.

Potbellied pigs, burros, roosters and goats have all served as mascots. Earlier this century a Thoroughbred named Hodge loved a talking crow who used to sit on a fence along the backstretch and yell, "Come on, Hodge! Come on, Hodge!"

Tall Tales

In the world of horses, the true tale is only a horse tail removed from the tall tale. Just hanging around stables, I have heard stories about horses that could slip the bolts on their stalls or get out of warm-up blankets, horses that loved to eat hats and buttons, and mischievous horses that would hide brushes and other grooming tools in the straw. A Thoroughbred called Le Danseur used to grab a rub-bag and play catch with his groom; Big Ben used to do the same with his groom's shoes.

No one can deny the extraordinary feats of the cutting horse, that marvel of western ranches. These quarter horses are neck-reined horses; to turn left, the rider simply applies the rein to the right side of the horse's neck. Cattle drives require horses capable of quick stops, tight turns and rapid acceleration: the quarter horse is brilliantly suited to the task. How brilliant? Cowboys would compete to tell you.

"Why, my cutting horse," one would say, "was once sighted riderless and alone working a herd of 1,500 cattle. And after he had cut out one big steer three times he finally lost his temper, grabbed that steer's tail in his teeth, gave it a twist and him a somersault. Then that horse sat on him for ten minutes."

There are tales of horses that faked injuries to avoid work, or cried tears to duck pack duty. One horse, it is claimed, could gallop backwards so the rider could let fly with two six-shooters at once.

Then there was Toro. How good a cutting horse was he? "Toro," said his rider, "could cut the baking powder out of a biscuit without breaking the crust."

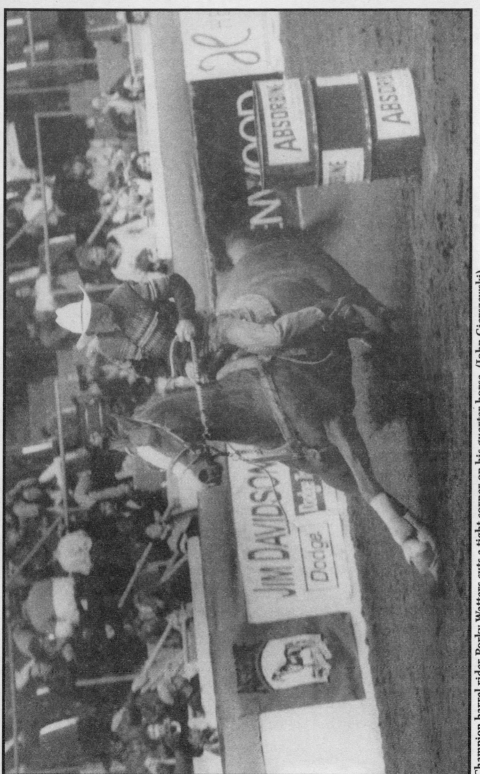

Champion barrel rider Porky Watters cuts a tight corner on his quarter horse. (John Gierszewski)

Horse Breakers, Horse Gentlers

Your young horse spooks the first time you show him bridle, bit and saddle. What to do? As a horse trainer, you have three options:

1. The on-your-knees way: Offer him carrots for life if he does what you ask.

2. The old way: Have a bronco-buster blindfold him, tie up his legs, sit on his head and generally terrorize him until he's willing to co-operate.

3. The new way: Win the horse's trust with a lot of tenderness, and win his respect with a little firmness.

The first way will not work.

The second way, the "breaking" of horses, is still practised on many western ranches today. It's called "sacking out." You tie the horse to a post and then put a weighted sack or tarpaulin on his back. Terrified, the horse might fight the sack for days. Then one leg is tied up to the horse's chest to prevent bucking. The saddle is put on, and eventually the horse is ridden. The aim is to "break" his spirit, make him see how hopeless it is to disobey his master.

But it's the third way, the new way, that's catching on. Many trainers now talk about "gentling" the horse. What is astonishing about this is how some young riders figured it out before the adults did, and how the "new" way isn't new at all.

A Greek cavalry officer named Xenophon (pronounced Zen´-uh-fawn) once wrote a book about training war horses. Today, more than 2,000 years later, it is still admired by many certified riding instructors.

Be firm but never harsh, he advised. It was fine to be determined in dealing with a horse, he said; it was not fine to lose your temper. "Never deal with him," Xenophon wrote, "when you are in a fit of passion."

Horse Whisperers

Today the grand old man of horse gentling is an elderly rancher in Gustine, California named Tom Dorrance. Some people call this fellow and others like him "horse whisperers" — for their uncanny ability to read the body language of horses. They listen to what the horse is saying, even the most subtle whisper.

Tom Dorrance began riding a cutting horse and moving cattle on his father's ranch in Oregon when he was only five years old. He would always be small, and for the first thirty years of his life he never weighed more than sixty kilograms. Dorrance had a boy's body and a man's job: dealing with horses capable of crushing his skull with one blow from a hoof.

"I couldn't manhandle a horse," he says. "I was often alone and far from home. If the horse got away, I'd have to walk." So Tom Dorrance, on his own and still very young, tried a different approach. It involved winning the horse's trust, and seeking to understand what the horse really meant when he lowered his head or whinnied or nudged Tom. Tom spent hours watching horses in the wild and in the paddock. Without ever reading Xenophon (he quit school before finishing grade eight) Tom came around to Xenophon's thinking all by himself.

Tom Dorrance thought he would try to see the world through the horse's eyes. Some cowboys today call him "the horse's lawyer" or "the patron saint of horses."

Eventually Dorrance wrote a book called *True Unity: Willing Communication Between Horse and Human*. It's about "reading" a horse, respecting a horse, and seeing riding as a dance in which one partner leads and one partner follows.

Along the way Dorrance has taught many students, who continue to pass on the art of gentling. One of them is Ray Hunt, a man in his seventies who still goes on the road demonstrating in clinics how to school a green horse. He does in a matter of hours what old bronco-busters took a week to do, or sometimes couldn't do at all. Hunt also wrote a book, *Think Harmony With Horses*, and dedicated it to the old master, Tom Dorrance. At one point in the book Hunt passes along this piece of useful advice: "The slower you do it, the quicker you'll find it."

Monty Roberts is another Californian and yet another horse gentler who has written a book, this one about his own life: *The Man Who Listens to Horses*. It's the story of a boy who loved horses and who eventually learned their language.

Roberts grew up on a rodeo grounds in Salinas. One of

his earliest memories is from age two: being up on a horse in his mother's arms as she gave riding lessons. When he was four he competed against sixteen-year-olds — and won. An accomplished rider by the age of ten, he got work in Hollywood as a stunt rider falling off galloping horses. He also became a double for famous Hollywood actors.

Elizabeth Taylor, for example, did much of her own riding in the film *National Velvet*. But the jockey in the racing scenes (considered too dangerous for Taylor) is actually Monty Roberts in a wig.

On the rodeo grounds, Monty would watch in horror as his father "sacked out" horses. Like Tom Dorrance, he began to wonder if there wasn't a better way. His father's attitude to horses was strict: Hurt the horse, he would say, before the horse hurts you.

Once when Monty was seven he spent three days in a ring with a young unbroken colt, just following it around and trying to earn the horse's trust. Finally the gelding began to follow him around, let himself be touched and even saddled. No sacking out. No tying to posts. No terror.

Monty proudly asked his father to observe what he had accomplished. But his father was outraged. He reacted as if his "wisdom" about breaking horses had been tossed in his face. For several minutes he beat his own son with a metre-long piece of stall chain. From that moment, Monty Roberts was determined that whatever way his father had used with horses, he would find another.

And he did. When he was about thirteen he and others would round up mustangs in the high desert of Nevada. Once he spent weeks alone up there, observing wild horses to see how they dealt with each other.

Monty spent a long time watching an older mare educate

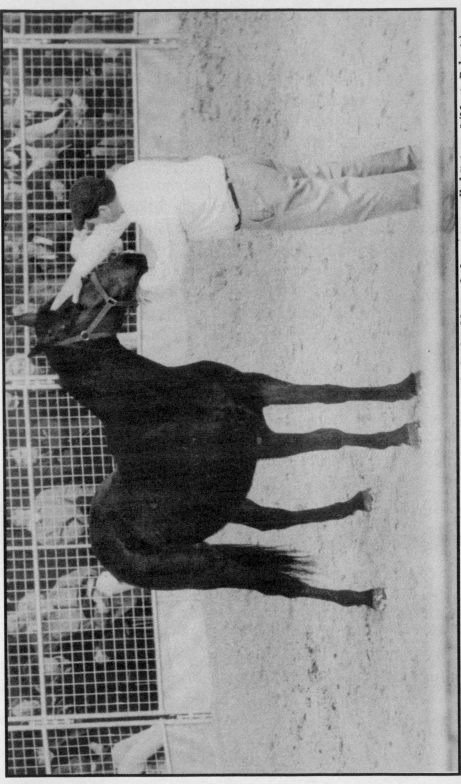

Monty Roberts has gained a horse's trust when the horse will follow him, or let his head be stroked — a stage called "join-up." (Monty Roberts)

a two-year-old colt who had the manners of a gang member. The colt was kicking mares and even biting foals, and by the fourth incident, the mare had had enough. A wild horse herd is like a high school, with the stallion the principal entrusted with protecting the students, and a senior mare his vice-principal in charge of day-to-day discipline. And that young colt was about to get some discipline.

She drove at the colt, knocked him down twice and expelled him from the herd. For a herd animal, this was severe punishment. The colt panicked, and to Monty's eyes, clearly begged to be let back into the herd. The mare did eventually let him back, and then did the strangest thing: she groomed him, fussed over him like he was a prize pupil. When he reoffended, he got the same treatment. Harsh at first, then welcoming. Pretty soon the colt knew the ropes.

But what really interested Monty was the body language of mare and colt. The mare would face him directly and stare. This, Monty saw, meant "Get lost!" By lowering his head to the ground, sticking out his tongue and making chewing motions, the colt was saying "Let me back in!"

Like many horse trainers, Monty Roberts is careful about making eye contact with young horses new to saddle and bridle. By watching mustangs he learned how to "converse" with a horse, and something about horse customs and manners. He has now gentled about 10,000 green or troubled horses, and all but a tiny few are willing to talk. Within thirty minutes and without a harsh word or action, Monty can bridle, saddle and mount an unbroken horse. It's a thing of beauty to watch. "A good trainer can hear a horse speak to him," he says. "A great trainer can hear him whisper."

How Not to Train Horses

If Monty Roberts is the man who listens to horses, there were many before him who heard not a word the horse was saying. This is the intriguing, and distressing, thing about the long history between horses and humans. From century to century, kindness would fall in and out of fashion. If there is a heaven for horses, may its pastures be home to colts who suffered at the hands of unthinking trainers.

In the sixteenth century an Englishman named Thomas Blundeville was advising horse trainers to set dogs on unco-operative horses. His other idea? Fix an angry cat to a pole and insert it between the horse's legs where it could scratch and bite the soft underbelly of any horse who offered trouble.

The nineteenth century, on the other hand, produced a man with keen insight into the way horses think. An Ohio farmer named John Solomon Rarey had been breaking horses the old way — along with almost every bone in his body. Then he began to ask around about alternatives. He read everything he could (maybe he read Xenophon), he talked to trainers, cowboys, circus folk. Eventually he came up with a system of breaking horses that relied at first on hobbling devices, then a lot of touching and gentle talking — much as Native American horse-breakers did on the plains.

Rarey became famous in Europe for calming so-called killer horses. Many observers believed a new era was about to begin, that the way humans trained horses would be changed forever.

They were wrong. Rarey had discovered by himself knowledge that already existed. But not only was the name of Rarey soon forgotten, so was the gift of his knowledge about gentling horses.

The Prince, the Horse, the Shadow

Horse trainers might never agree on the philosophy of teaching skills to a horse, but on this they might: schooling a horse is about paying attention to particulars. Find the key to that horse.

More than 2,000 years ago, the story goes, a young Macedonian prince named Alexander was paying attention when his father, the king, was considering whether to buy a huge black horse. Nobles had gathered to watch this horse put through his paces. But the horse was a fury, and no one could even mount him. His own grooms stayed well clear of his flashing hoofs and menacing teeth. The price being asked for the horse was high, so clearly the owner thought him superior.

The king was angry that such a vile-tempered animal was being offered to the royal family, and he ordered the horse taken away. But amid all the prancing and pawing of the great black horse, the twelve-year-old prince had noticed something. "What a horse they are losing," he said with some sadness, while regretting aloud the handlers' lack of skill.

The king, like many parents, said as much as "So you think you can do better?" The prince was so certain that he could, he offered to pay the full price of this seemingly vicious horse if he was unable to tame him. Historians suggest that the price being asked was thirteen talents, or more than $10,000 in modern currency. A lot of money, even for a prince. Imagine the embarrassment if he failed.

Alexander approached the horse, took him by the bridle and turned him to face the sun. This was the key. The horse feared his own shadow, and simply pointing him to the sun calmed him. Alexander spoke softly to him, stroked him, then mounted him. They took off in a gallop, which alarmed the king, but soon they were back. The unruly horse had met his rider.

The king wept with joy, for he saw that his son was destined for greatness. "Macedonia," he said, "is too small for thee." The king was right: Prince Alexander became Alexander the Great. He would conquer much of the known world a few hundred years before Christ was born. The horse was Bucephalus.

Bucephalus would kneel before his master and be mounted, and into battle they would go. After many campaigns he died at the age of thirty, an unusual life span for a horse in those days. During the final battle in India, horse and general waded into the thick of the enemy, and the horse took spears in both his neck and flank, but still managed to turn and get Alexander to safety before dying.

Alexander was overcome with grief, and later named a city after Bucephalus. "He was as dear to his master," wrote one historian, "as Alexander was terrible to the barbarians."

Some historians suggest that the ancients typically saw horses as weapons in war, took no particular pleasure in riding, and felt no real affection for their mounts. If so, Bucephalus was clearly an exception. All this because a young boy, a gentler before his time, listened to his horse.

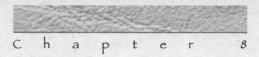

Pony Power

Ponies — often feisty and headstrong — typically offer a child that first contact with riding. At the farms of some world-class riders and trainers, you will sometimes find in one stall an old hairy creature sleeping away his days. Some ancient pony, a rider's first love, has earned himself a cushy retirement. This is the enduring power of ponies.

In Praise of Ponies

Experts say that a pony has a certain defined look and is typically under fourteen and a half hands. Pony lovers and fanciers — like Dick and Adele Rockwell — say it's quite easy to distinguish between pony and horse: the pony is smarter, and inch for inch can far outjump a horse.

At their rolling farm north of Toronto, Ontario, the Rockwells have been raising and training Welsh ponies for more than forty years. Their living room is like a pony museum: the shelves strain under the weight of trophies from pony shows, and from pony sculptures and paintings. From

Pokey is 26 years old. A patient older pony can be the best teacher for a new rider. (Karen Briggs)

floor to ceiling, the walls are pink with ribbons. Around Dick and Adele's pony farm, they sing the praises of ponies. Even the mischievous ones.

Flyaway, for example, a four-time grand champion sire at the Royal Winter Fair, was once found in a pasture with fillies. Dick accused Adele of failing to lock the gate, then returned Flyaway to his own paddock. Minutes later, Adele noticed Flyaway back with the fillies, and this time she tossed the blame back at Dick, who once more restored Flyaway to his paddock. Then both Dick and Adele watched in fascination as Flyaway methodically bumped the fence with his rear end. With each bump the slide would move . . . until the gate would open about five minutes later. In the end, the only way to keeping Flyaway from "flying away" was two locks — one vertical and one horizontal.

Protected by Ponies

In Britain the Pony Club came into existence after some military officers, seeing how the horse was fast disappearing as a force in war, feared that horsemanship skills would be lost. They created the Pony Club after the First World War to ensure that younger generations would know about posting and half-halts and flying changes.

Colonel R.S Timmins launched a Canadian chapter of the Pony Club in 1934. When he went off to war in 1939 Adele Rockwell succeeded him. The club would meet in Toronto's Don Valley, and some of its members would grow up to be notables in the horse world. Ian Millar, who would later ride the legendary Big Ben to two world championships in show jumping, was a Pony Club kid. So were Tom Gayford, Torchy Millar, Jim Elder, Norm Elder — familiar names to horse lovers, and Canadian Olympic champions all.

Adele remembers one boy from those Pony Club days. As she described him, the boy seemed like a character in a Charles Dickens novel. Maybe he never had to plead, like Oliver Twist, for more gruel, but he did know poverty. His father was blind, his mother took in washing, and if he could pay the membership fee — at that time seventy-five cents — that was only because he had a paper route.

At all those Pony Club meetings — when Adele would bring in vets and blacksmiths, and show films — young Brian was paying attention. He eventually got a job at Woodbine racetrack in Toronto, walking horses after workouts. "Hot-walking," they call it. One time a trainer had given up on a horse as too crippled, but Brian begged for a chance to rehabilitate the Thoroughbred. He did, and the horse won $300 — "more money," said Adele, "than [Brian] had seen in his life."

Years later Adele saw Brian's name in a newspaper. He had been named lead trainer at a big track in California.

Pony Clubs like the one Adele led are still flourishing across Canada, and in the United States. Riding a pony remains a great way to introduce a child to the world of horses.

The Pony Express

History leaves no doubt that ponies are remarkable creatures. As couriers, for example, ponies always delivered what was asked of them.

The U.S. Post Office commemorated the eightieth and hundredth anniversaries of the founding of the Pony Express by issuing stamps. Though the Pony Express existed for just eighteen months, images of ponies racing flat-out across the plains still live in our imaginations, over 130 years later.

On April 3, 1860, while a great crowd looked on, a bay mare left Pony Express headquarters in St. Joseph, Missouri to begin the first mad dash across the continent. History does not record the pony's name, but she must have been happy to go. Hawkers and souvenir-hunters, aware of what an historic occasion this was, had been plucking hair from her tail to make rings and watch chains.

Pony Express mounts were small (usually under fourteen hands) and often weighed about 320 kilograms. Usually they were mustangs rounded up on the plains, or ponies purchased from Native tribes. The riders were astonishingly young — under eighteen years of age, and some only fifteen. They were short and wiry, jockey-size, and the Company made them swear never to drink to excess or to curse, never to treat the animals cruelly and never to act other than as a gentleman. Anyone who broke the oath would be fired without pay.

Little more than boys, these young men had names that belonged in novels of the Old West: Sawed-Off Cumbo, Deadwood Dick, Yank Little. Some went by only one name, like Whipsaw or Boston.

One rider's name was Johnny Frye, and if you believe this

far-fetched tale, then it's thanks to Johnny we have dough-nuts. He had made something of a name for himself as a jockey at local races. Some young women had noticed him and would wait for him along the way with cookies and cakes in hand. He would grab the cookies as he raced by, but his admirers saw how he struggled to hold their offerings in one hand and ride with the other. Why not, one young lady said to herself, put a hole in the middle of her baked offering? That way Johnny could slide a thumb through it and still keep both hands on the reins. Thus, the story goes, the doughnut was born.

Whatever Pony Express couriers actually ate, they took it on the fly. Riders changed horses every 16 or 32 kilometres and might have to gallop 125 to 200 kilometres a day. The aim was to get the mail pouch, or *mochila*, from St. Joseph, Missouri to Sacramento, California — some 3,400 kilometres away — in eleven days.

Riding for Your Life

Despite the oath never to mistreat ponies, riders often had to ride for their lives, and the ponies paid the price. There were the usual obstacles — deserts and snowy mountain passes to cross, dust storms and blizzards, biting insects, bears and cougars, and sometimes even Native warriors to fight. One rider, Joseph Wintle, was chased for many kilometres before finally reaching the relay station where his pursuers turned away. The poor horse who had saved Joseph's life, however, died on the spot.

Sometimes towns under siege had to rely on Pony Express riders to fetch the cavalry. In Nevada in 1860, the Pah Utes were accused of a murder, and half the posse sent out to punish them were killed in an ambush. The fearful citizens of Carson City converted a hotel into a fort and prepared for war. But help would only come if the Pony Express could get through.

When "Pony Bob" Haslam rode into Carson City, he found every available horse out with the doomed posse. He fed his poor pony and coaxed another 125 kilometres out of him, but the rider at the next relay station was too frightened of the Pah Utes and refused to carry the mail. Pony Bob galloped on with a fresh pony, and by the time he got to Cold Spring he had gone 316 kilometres without a rest. At Cold Spring he rested a mere eight hours. The same unfortunate pony had to continue because the station had been attacked, its keeper killed and all the horses taken. By the end of his long gallop, Pony Bob had gone 633 kilometres and had been in the saddle almost continuously for thirty-six hours.

The record for long-distance riding among Pony Express riders, though, was claimed by William Frederick Cody, known later as Buffalo Bill. Young William started riding for the Express when he was fifteen and already a fine rider. Impatient with the short safe runs he was assigned in the beginning, he yearned for the longer, riskier rides. He got his wish: the sometimes deadly 193-kilometre run from Red Buttes to Three Crossings.

On one occasion, William Cody arrived to find his replacement dead, so he rode another pony west and then other ponies all the way back east again — a virtually non-stop dash of 640 kilometres.

By the time he was hired by the railroad to supply buffalo meat to its construction crews, Cody had made a name for himself. The legend of Buffalo Bill was born.

The Pony Express was short-lived. As fast as the ponies

were, they were no match for the telegraph line. But the reputation created by the hardy ponies and brave riders of the Pony Express lives on more than a century later.

Ancient Mail

The Pony Express wasn't the only postal system to have used ponies. In ancient Persia 2,400 years ago, Cyrus the Great — the so-called King of the World, so vast was his empire — might have been the first to establish a system of conveying royal messages by setting up posting stations twenty-five kilometres apart.

A Greek traveller named Herodotus who saw the system operate was much impressed. "Neither snow nor rain nor heat nor gloom of night stays these couriers from swift completion of their appointed rounds," he wrote. His words would be adopted as the unofficial motto of the American post office, and are still etched in stone outside its New York headquarters.

Genghis Khan, the fierce Mongol ruler, did something similar — employing 20,000 horses and 10,000 relay stations to keep in touch with the far-flung reaches of his empire.

Maria, and a Pony Named Merlin

A young rider named Maria Simpson told me about her mount, a chunky seven-year-old Welsh cob named Merlin who has as much pony in him as horse. He is extraordinarily kind and mannered with Maria, feisty with everyone else. Maria, you see, has cerebral palsy. Merlin must be sensitive enough to respond to the slight leg squeeze that Maria is capable of, as well as her voice commands. She loves that horse; calls him "a sweetheart" and "a character and a half."

Hippo-therapy (using horses to help disabled riders) sometimes works best when the rider turns and rides backwards. (Rick Buncombe)

"But when my coach gets on him," says Maria, "he can be as wild as a bucking bronco. When I get on him, he relaxes. He knows it's me and that he can't be silly."

What riding offers Maria is almost beyond words. "It's a freedom," she says. "In the trot and canter I get that fast feeling. I can't run but the horse can do it for me. I'm doing something an able-bodied person can do." And by all accounts she does it very well, and even competes in international dressage events.

The ancient Greeks used to put injured soldiers on horseback; the rhythm of the walking horse was found to be therapeutic. Today, groups all over North America offer riding for kids with special needs. Jessica Clarke, assistant equestrian director at the Community Association for Riding for the Disabled in Toronto, says they use specially trained horses who respond to voice commands or subtle aids.

"The list of benefits to disabled kids is as long as your arm," she told me. "The bone structure of the horse's pelvis is very similar to our own. So when the horse walks, his pelvis moves in much the same way as the rider's does. It means that a disabled rider, perhaps for the first time, may have her own pelvis mobilized. That's where all the benefits of riding begin. Riding often improves the rider's balance, posture, mobility and upper body function. Sometimes it helps kids walk. I know of at least one case where a young boy who took up riding learned to walk hanging on to the arm of someone else; he couldn't do that before. It continually blows my mind what riding can do for a child's muscle tone and self-confidence. Riding even helps speech — and no one understands why. It's just extraordinary."

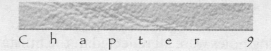

Wild Horses

A wild horse herd on the move is as stirring a sight now as it must have been 6,000 years ago, and even today still symbolizes freedom and high spirit. But in the 1800s on the plains, some cattle ranchers called wild horses "jugheads," a dismissive term that justified their cruel treatment. In 1919 the American government declared the need to "rid the range of these worthless horses." In Australia, wild horses were "brumbies" — "a very weed among animals."

But who is to say that free-range horses are worthless? At one point during a week-long ride in the badlands of central Wyoming, my friends and I cantered alongside a low ridge. We did not know that on the other side of the ridge, running parallel to us, was a herd of twenty-five mustangs. When the ridge flattened, there the wild ones were.

We whooped like children when school is out for the summer. It was a moment out of a dream, too breathtaking to be real. We were literally galloping on the plains with wild horses.

Only fifteen metres away, they were strikingly handsome. Generous spring rains, rich grass in the lowlands and plenty of drinking holes were all reflected in the mustangs' glossy coats. The black stallion, the painted and chestnut mares, the foals — all looked oiled and slick, as if freshly groomed. Long manes and tails flying, they matched us easily stride for stride, then put on a burst before crossing the dirt road ahead of us and running alongside us there for a time. Finally they peeled off and disappeared over a hillside.

We saw many wild horses that week — grazing in the next valley, high on a ridge at sunset, on distant tablelands. But never did we get so close as we did that day, never did we experience so clearly the wild horses' playfulness and exuberance — the pure joy of romping over thick sagebrush in the high desert.

Two Million Wild Horses

These mustangs are the remnants of magnificent herds that once roamed the central plains of North America. The savannah that nourished the buffalo also fed horses liberated during the sixteenth century from the Spanish who had colonized parts of Latin America. The wild horses grew steadily in number and kept spreading north and west into the territory of their ancestors. By some estimates, two million wild horses moved freely on this continent in the early 1800s. By the late 1960s, however, their numbers had dwindled to a mere 17,000. Where did all those horses go? Who or what killed them?

We did. As settlers pushed west and established ranches, wild horses got in the way. In the late 1800s, cattle and sheep were the flowers; wild horses were the weeds, and they were mowed down like so many dandelions. Wild horses competed with livestock for grass, stallions trampled fence lines and stole ranchers' mares. In the early 1900s the free territory

A Stampede of Wild Horses. Engraving. (Corbis-Bettmann)

open to horses rapidly diminished. Like the whale, like the buffalo, the wild horse was just one more magnificent creature on the path to extinction.

But the story does not end there — largely due to one remarkable woman by the name of Velma Johnston, who knew what it was to live as an outcast. In 1923, at the age of eleven, Velma was stricken with polio. Some classmates teased her mercilessly for her disability, but she found comfort in poetry and drawing and in the animals on her parents' ranch.

Velma Johnston almost single-handedly saved the mustangs. One morning in 1950 when she was driving to work in Reno, Nevada, a truck hauling horses cut in front of her car. She noticed a stream of blood flowing from inside the truck. Shocked, she followed the van and watched from behind bushes as a yearling was trampled between terrified stallions packed like sardines in trucks and corrals outside a slaughterhouse. That terrible scene would haunt her for the rest of her life, a life she would dedicate to a better fate for wild horses — animals she loved in spirit but not necessarily in the flesh. Ironically, Velma was allergic to horses.

Like many who take up a cause, she began writing letters of protest to politicians and bureaucrats. But Wild Horse Annie — as Velma Johnston would eventually be called, first by her enemies and then by her friends — was more persistent than most. She blew the whistle on wild horse slaughter.

Cruel Round-Up

Cattle and sheep farmers would not share precious land with wild horses (and who can blame them?). Pet food manufacturers saw in the wild horses a cheap source of meat. And so cowboys called "mustangers" rounded up the poor horses — aided by airplanes.

Velma described it in a letter: "The mustangs are driven at breakneck speed by planes from their meagre refuge in the rough and barren rimrock onto flatlands or dry lake beds. There the chase is taken up by hunters standing on fast-moving pickup trucks, and the exhausted mustangs . . . many of them carrying bullet wounds to make them run the faster, are easy victims for ropers."

The wild horse was lassoed, with a heavy truck tire acting as anchor. The mustanger tied the horse's feet and the exhausted creature was pulled up a rough plank ramp onto a stock truck, where the ropes were removed and he was prodded to his feet. The act of hauling the horse up the ramp would often have left the horse injured, and always badly frightened.

But the horse's terror had only just begun. The slaughterhouse was typically many hours away, perhaps in another state or even in another country. (Horses were sometimes shipped to Canadian factories.) Some horses packed into trucks were already crippled and hurt. Left behind to die were young colts, or horses too badly injured to load.

A great long war of words ensued when these details were made public. Nine years after Velma Johnston first followed that slaughterhouse truck, the U.S. Congress passed what became known as the Wild Horse Annie Law. Using vehicles and polluting water holes to capture wild horses were both banned.

Later, in 1971, Wild Horse Annie and her many allies got another law passed. This one protected wild horses and burros from capture, harassment or death. Protective ranges were declared in Montana, Nevada, Wyoming and several other states. One in Colorado was dedicated to the memory of Wild Horse Annie.

Today the International Society for the Protection of Mustangs and Burros, which Velma Johnston helped found, oversees an adoption program. The government occasionally removes some wild horses to control their numbers, and members of the public are invited to "adopt" these horses. In principle, it's a good idea and often works well. But too many of these horses still end up at meat-packing plants — often because the owner lacked the skill or patience required to gentle a wild horse.

In Canada a similar adoption program kicked in when government authorities announced their plans in 1994 to slaughter the 1,200 horses that had been roaming freely since 1930 on the Canadian Forces Base near Medicine Hat, Alberta. Thousands of people objected and asked to take the horses. Some paid $350 each for as many as twenty-five horses — just for the privilege of watching the herd roam freely on their land.

Gentling Horses, Gentling Humans

Sometimes people want to ride their adopted mustangs, and sometimes the job of training them falls to convicts. Why convicts? Many horse people say the horse is a wonderful teacher, and what the wild horse teaches prisoners is the wisdom of patience, gentleness and trust. This unusual pairing of horses and convicts offers practical skills that the prisoners might use after their release, plus lessons in humanity that might just keep them out of prison. The gentling of horses is also about the gentling of humans, and some of the prisoners have caught a little horse fever themselves. Over the past nine years, 4,000 wild horses have been gentled in Wild Horse Inmate Programs in four American states.

Tom Chenoweth, a horse trainer with thirty years of experience, oversees an inmate program in California. Prisoners, he says, have no choice but to go slow with a wild horse whose first experience of a human — being dragged into the prison yard on the end of a choking rope — has been brutally imprinted on his brain.

"All the animals want is to escape," says Tom. "The last thing they want is to be touched. You have to wait for them to approach you. You've just got to learn to talk to a horse right. It's all about understanding."

It may take weeks before the horse lets a human close enough to groom, halter, bridle and saddle him. Injuries sometimes occur, but even that is seen as a useful lesson for tough-guy cons short on respect. The patience required is extraordinary, and any convict who loses his temper with a horse can undo weeks of hard work and have to start over. But at the end of all that work is a fine horse.

"Once they know you they're incredibly affectionate," says a government official involved in the program. "They're not always pretty horses, but they're perfect horses: they're horses as nature designed them, not as humans have bred them."

In fact, one reason to preserve the wild horse is as a gene pool to be dipped into as needed. As Karen Sussman (president of the organization founded by Wild Horse Annie) put it, "We're breeding pretty and beautiful horses, but pretty and beautiful may not last." Studies show that wild horses are more genetically diverse than any other breed of horse. Nature weeds out the weak, the lame, the unwary: those left are tough enough to endure harsh winters and summer drought, and to resist disease.

Sable Island's Hardy Horses

In Canada few wild horses remain. One place where they can still be found in significant numbers is on Sable Island, about a hundred kilometres off the east coast of Nova Scotia. A sandy spit some forty-eight kilometres long and just a kilometre and a half wide, the island has no trees to offer the horses shade in summer. Their only food consists of coarse dune grasses, wild pea plants and low shrubs. From winter gales, from bone-chilling fog there is almost no shelter.

The several hundred wild horses who live on Sable Island (*sable* is the French word for sand) are one of the few remaining wild herds in the world which has been spared human intervention. The Sable Island horses are also — no coincidence — among the toughest horses in the world. How they originally got to the island remains a matter of debate, though they may have been survivors of shipwrecks.

Sable Island horses have the look of north African Barbs. They are as hardy as any on the planet. We should let nature continue its course on the island. One day on the mainland we may have need of such quality bloodlines.

But will the world's wild horses endure? Pressed into sometimes small ranges today, wild horse herds may grow too numerous for the territory. Horses may starve if their numbers are not reduced, and they can do great harm to delicate ecosystems.

The eternal problem is the sharing of land. And so far, we humans have put our needs and desires ahead of wild creatures. We still prize the wild horse, still thrill to see a herd's fleet crossing of the plains. But maybe not nearly enough.

A Mustang Called Utah

Susan Blair Seward has described in a story how she came to own a mustang called Utah, a fiery little horse rounded up for adoption and later brought to a horse shelter in Leesburg, Virginia. Seward had always been something of a horse snob, used to riding sleek Thoroughbred hunters. Her friends had always dismissed mustangs: like the alley cat and the SPCA mutt, such horses lacked breeding. But something about rugged little Utah touched her.

Seward never regretted buying Utah in 1993. She was struck by his toughness. She had to smile when her friends' pedigreed mounts succumbed to foot problems, breathing disorders and other common ailments unknown to Utah and his wild kin.

Seward wrote with eloquence about how only the strong survive: "Utah's flint-hard hoofs, alert, wide-set eyes and iron constitution are no accident; they are the creation of the perfect by the divine."

She and Utah take great joy in their gallops across enormous fields, with the wind drowning out everything but the thunder of his hoofs. But sometimes Seward regrets confining a creature born in freedom. A little sadly, she will take out a map of the state of Utah and trace with her finger the tiny town of Milford where the mustang caught his last glimpse of home, "his big world of hills, rocks and sky."

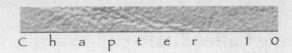
Horses of Myth and Legend

Before riding into battle, the Navajo warrior would whisper into the ear of his horse. He was really talking to himself, so much did he feel at one with his horse. "Be lively," he would whisper. "You and I are going into a dangerous business, my horse. Be brave when you go to war and nothing will happen; we will come back safely."

Late in the 1800s the U.S. army crushed the last resistance of the Navajo. Take away their horses, the army realized, and you destroy their spirit of defiance. The horseless Navajo were confined to Fort Sumner in New Mexico, where they went on conducting their religious rites. One ritual, called the Enemy Way, was one they had long performed on horseback — but now they had no horses. They improvised.

The Navajo decorated long sticks and painted them to represent the different colours of horses; they stuck crude horse-heads on one end and then "rode" these sticks in their

110

ceremony, much like the children of pioneers used to ride hobby horses.

Imagine how these proud people must have longed to ride the plains on horseback as they had done for centuries. The Navajo rode their stick horses, they said, so that one day when they were free — for surely they would not live like this for long? — their children would once more have horses.

The connection between horses and humans is special, and, for some individuals, almost spiritual. As a Sioux medicine man named Lame Deer once wrote,

> **We had no word**
> **for the strange animal**
> **we got from the**
> **white man — the horse.**
> **So we called it** *ŝunka wakan,*
> **'holy dog.' For bringing us the horse**
> **we could almost forgive you for**
> **bringing us whiskey.**
> **Horses make a landscape**
> **look more beautiful.**

Many ancient peoples created enduring myths and stories to explain this gift of the gods. An old Piegan woman who died in 1880 told this story to Montana pioneers. She was called Sikey-kio (Black Bear), and children in her foothills village might have heard her tell the story of "How the Piegans Got Their First Horses":

One evening a daughter of the chief saw a bright star and muttered, "If that star were a young man, I would marry him." Next day a fine young man appeared to her on the trail. He was the star, and if she closed her eyes he would take her to his star world. There she lived happily with her new husband, the son of the chief.

There were good roots to eat up there, but she was forbidden to dig one in particular. Curiosity overcame her and she dug deep with a pointed stick to get it, so deep she made a hole in the sky world. She could see the earth world and her village far below. It made her sad to see her old family, so her husband made a long rope of buffalo hides and gently lowered her to the earth world. There she bore a son, but later died from a plague, so an uncle cared for the boy.

Up in the sky world, the great chief saw how poor and hungry the people were down below. He went to the boy — his own grandson — and asked him to bring wet clay. The clay grew and finally moved. Then the Great Chief called a council of the trees, birds and animals, for he was their ruler.

"I have made a horse for my grandson," he told them, "an animal for him to ride. And it will also carry his burdens. Now each of you will give me of your wisdom, that this horse may be perfect." The pine tree contributed a tail, the fir tree a mane. The turtle offered hoofs, the elk gave his great size, the cottonwood fashioned a saddle. The buffalo gave a hair bridle; the snake's gift was straps, the wolf's a fur robe.

The boy now mounted the horse and rode back to his people, who were astonished and then envious of the colts that followed. For they had none. The boy became a young man and one day he told his uncle to take the tribe to the edge of a nearby lake. He said he would be going away, but not before turning every fish in the lake into a horse. The people were to catch the horses as they came from the lake. "But you, uncle," he said, "are to catch none until my old mare comes from the water. Catch her and her alone."

When the young man rode the mare into the lake, the water began to bubble and foam. Horses by the hundreds emerged from the water and many were captured, but countless others escaped and formed wild herds on the plains.

Last out was the feeble old mare, and though the people laughed at him the uncle did as his nephew had told him. He tied her to a stake by his lodge. That night, as the moon came over the hills the old mare neighed three times and thousands of colts came from the woods and surrounded the uncle's lodge. He was now rich in horses. That is how the Great Chief gave horses to the Piegans.

The White Stallion

Imagine the comfort that Native Americans took from the horse. The Great Spirit was clearly looking after them, for he had given them this gift on four legs. But the pioneers who crossed the plains had stories of their own, stories of a white stallion. The sightings were offered as true, and maybe some were, but they have the feel of myth. One story, especially, seemed designed to comfort pioneers as they crossed forbidding territory.

German pioneers heading west through Texas in covered wagons had tied a little girl called Gretchen onto the back of an old mare, who then wandered off in search of grass. According to the little girl, a white mustang led this mare back to his own herd. There the stallion cut the ropes that held her in place and lifted her up by the collar, as a mother cat would lift a kitten. Later, after Gretchen had rested, the white stallion put her back on the mare and instructed the mare to return the girl to her family camp. The mustang stallion had the bearing of a prince, said Gretchen, but "something about him" kept her calm.

The white stallion figures in horse myths and legends the world over. (Marilyn Kelley)

The legend of the white stallion grew. He was always noble in spirit. His endurance, speed and intelligence had no equal, and those who caught even a glimpse of him remembered his beauty and grace, his flowing mane and tail. Every youth dreamed of capturing and taming the white steed.

Wild horse traders tried to catch him. One story has a hundred men on their best mounts trapping him in a canyon and chasing him round and round in a circle, until each horse was exhausted. The white mustang, though, was just toying with those horses. He scaled the cliff and disappeared over the top.

In a tale that dates from the late 1800s, the steed finally meets his death. A small fortune was offered for his capture, and so he was tracked relentlessly. Near the Rio Grande, he was finally trapped by three vaqueros who all roped him at the same time. They staked him to a spot by water and grass but he refused any of it and after ten days lay down and died. The great stallion, true to legend, chose death over loss of liberty.

Pegasus

Notice that horses of myth and legend are often white? The ancient Greeks believed that in the heavens with the gods lived Pegasus, an immortal and winged snowy-white horse.

The father of Pegasus was Poseidon, god of the sea. His mother was Medusa — a once-beautiful woman turned into a gorgon, with bulging eyes and snakes for hair. A hero named Perseus cut off her head, and when drops of her blood fell into the sea-foam, Poseidon used them to create a winged steed with unimaginable speed: Pegasus.

Next Poseidon created the horse, without the fancy

Perseus rides Pegasus, while carrying the head of Medusa. (The Bettmann Archive)

wings, for mere mortals to ride. As human history unfolded down through the centuries, each new culture would have its own gods, its own sense of heaven. And in many of those cultures the horse — and often the white horse — was right up there with the gods.

• In Ireland lived Ler, a kind of Poseidon. His son Manannán mac Ler was the patron saint of sailors. (In Gaelic, Ler means "the sea," mac means "son of.") His horse Splendid Mane was swifter than the wind and as fast on water as on land. When a storm breaks over the sea off Ireland, the breakers are said to be the white horses of Manannán mac Ler.

• According to Hindu legend, the god Vishnu has descended into the world nine times in various animal forms. The tenth visit will be the last. Vishnu waits in the sky seated on a white and winged horse, who is poised with one hoof in the air. When that hoof descends, the earth will cease to exist.

• The ancients of India and of Greece offered sacrifices to the gods, and what better animal to sacrifice than one they valued? Still, they could not quite bring themselves to spill equine blood. Instead, they would select white steeds and drive them into the sea, where they drowned.

Heavenly Horses

The horse was busy up there in the heavens. The ancient Norse, Poles, Chinese, Greeks and Persians all believed that the horse drew the sun daily across the sky. Only the horse, they reasoned, was strong enough.

Baltic people once believed that horses had an afterlife. Ancient Lithuanians used to bury horses all tacked up, as if ready to ride; some were buried in cemeteries meant only for horses. Many cultures buried horses with their chiefs, so the ruler had transportation in the next world. (Unfortunately, sometimes grooms and horses still very much alive were entombed with the dead king!)

But the pagan tradition of horse sacrifice faded as the Christian tradition grew stronger. New tales emerged, like this one, which explains why even today people hang horseshoes for good luck on barns and houses: St. Dunstan, a bishop in early England, once saw the devil in a horse he was shoeing. To frustrate the devil's plan, St. Dunstan made Satan promise never to disturb a building on which its owner had hung a horseshoe — which had to be mounted open side up, so the luck could not drain out.

The ancient Chinese thought magic steeds carried their dead emperors up to heaven. The Huns worshipped the skull of a horse, and believed the shoulder blade of a horse could tell your fortune. The Vikings claimed that the head of a horse possessed supernatural powers, and that to put a curse on an enemy you simply beheaded a horse, set the skull on a pole and aimed it at the victim. The curse had more power when the skull's mouth was propped open.

Perhaps the head of a horse did possess strange powers. Sir Robert de Shurland, a thirteenth-century knight, once swam his horse far out to sea to beg forgiveness from his king, who was passing by on a ship. It seems the knight had buried a priest alive, but the king still forgave him.

Back on the beach, the exhausted horse hauled himself and his rider out of the sea. An old woman told Sir Robert that although his magnificent horse had saved his life, it would also cost him his life. The ungrateful knight immediately lopped off the horse's head with his sword. An end to the horse, he thought, would put an end to the woman's prophecy.

A year later Sir Robert was walking across the same beach when he came across the horse's skull. When he kicked it in contempt, a bone splinter entered his foot. Sir Robert died from the infection — just as the old woman said he would, but not in a way he could ever have imagined. Even in death, the horse had power.

Epilogue

Maybe now you better understand our powerful attraction to horses. I have told many stories, because stories sometimes capture truth better than anything. This book began with the story of Colonel, the gentle draft horse. Let it end with the stories of a boy named Henry and two girls named Maxine and Melissa, and how horses enriched their lives.

When Henry Blake, a British horseman and writer, was only one year old, his father bought a black Thoroughbred gelding named Masterpiece. The horse would kick at anyone who came close. One day panic gripped the household because little Henry had gone missing. Finally they found him — not just in the stall with Masterpiece, but right under Masterpiece's legs.

The fiery horse was quite content to have him there, and fought any attempt by Henry's parents to remove him. The toddler was finally tempted out of the stall by candy. For a long time after that, Henry would seek refuge in that stall under Masterpiece if his parents or babysitter got stern with him. The horse, again, as guardian. Henry would grow up to be a noted horseman and a writer; his special interest was the language of horses.

Foals for Maxine

When Maxine Kumin was a little girl growing up in Philadelphia, Pennsylvania, she preferred the smell of manure mixed with wood shavings to that of perfume. She still does. Maxine would grow up to be a writer and win the Pulitzer Prize for Poetry, which is a bit like winning a gold medal at the Olympics. Maxine never lost her love for horses; she still writes about horses, raises horses, rides horses.

She once called the foals who arrive every year in her barn "the best present of my middle age." And she remembers a favourite book from her childhood, *Silver Snaffles*. It's about a little girl who learns a magic password that lets her, for awhile, into the world of speaking horses.

Maxine found the ending almost unbearably sad. Some forty years later she chanced upon the book in a library, reread it there, and wept again. But the experience taught her to understand a little better that thing called horse fever. The bond between girls and horses, she says, is about closeness. And sometimes it lasts a lifetime.

You can count on horses, says Maxine, and that's what draws girls, especially, to horses. A young girl often discovers horses at a time in her life when it seems there's little she can count on. Her best girlfriend may turn against her; her boyfriend may admire her one day and forget about her the next; brothers and sisters can be quarrelsome, parents can be demanding, teachers can grow suddenly distant. "By comparison," Maxine tells us, "the horse is predictable, manageable, kindly. The horse is the one stable thing in a fickle climate."

Maxine once asked Julia, a twelve-year-old girl who helped around her barn, why she loved riding horses. "It gives you a sense of freedom," Julia replied. "You're sort of out of touch because you're higher up than anybody else." She loved the warm feeling she got by putting the horses away for the night. "You know you've made them feel cozy and secure."

Horses Will Listen

It works the other way too. Horses can make humans feel cozy and secure. Jodi Davies has been riding since the age of four. "Horses will listen," she says. "They may not understand but they listen. It's a challenge to be in control of such a great animal, and when you are, it makes you feel very confident."

Melissa Girouard, another young rider, told me about a time she needed Buddy, the black pony in her life. She had just received some shattering news from home — "the saddest day of my life," she called it. Perhaps instinctively, she went to the stable. Imagine the scene. Melissa standing, the pony on a lunge line trotting a circle around her, the tears streaming down Melissa's face.

Buddy stopped and went to her, and when she assured him with a pat to the star on his forehead that he was not the problem, he licked the salty tears from her face. "Somehow," Melissa said, "he knew I needed comfort. And that was what he gave me as he tickled my cheek with his whiskers."

Just being around a horse, touching or feeding a horse can lift our spirits. Getting close to one horse can make you feel connected to the great family of horses, even to horses long gone. Horses like Ruffian and Comanche, Mancha and Gato, Bucephalus, Clever Hans and Halla.

Those with the fever, those born to ride, know who they

are. For them the sound of a horse neighing will always be music, the smell of horse leather will always be sweet, the rush of a gallop will always be welcome, like a cool breeze under trees on still summer days.

Bernard Clark

Lawrence Scanlan first encountered horses during summers at his grandparents' farm. Since then he has become what he calls "a capable rider, or at least an adventurous one." He has ridden in the badlands of Wyoming, and plans to visit Peru to ride the famous Paso Fino horse. His dream is to have horses on the land he owns in Prince Edward County, Ontario.

Lawrence's love of riding is matched by his fondness for books. His home office is lined with pine shelves stacked floor to ceiling with books, so that when he's writing he is always surrounded by them. He is a journalist and freelance magazine writer, and the winner of three national magazine awards.

Lawrence edited and wrote the introduction for Monty Roberts's *The Man Who Listens to Horses*, and is writing a new book called *Wild About Horses*. He lives with his wife and son in Camden East, Ontario.

Other books by Lawrence Scanlan:

Riding High, co-written with equestrian Ian Millar

Big Ben

Heading Home: On Starting a New Life in a Country Place